Cover design by Tim Larson
Cover design resources from Nancy Hamilton Myers
Inside design by Aaron Troia

Copyright © 2008 by
Pacific Press® Publishing Association
Printed in the United States of America

You can obtain additional copies of this book by calling toll-free 1-800-765-6955 or by
visiting http://www.adventistbookcenter.com.

Library of Congress Cataloging-in-Publication Data

Thomas, Jerry D., 1959–
    Blessings : a contemporary adaptation of Ellen White's classic work
Thoughts from the Mount of Blessing / Jerry D. Thomas.
        p. cm.
    ISBN 13: 978-0-8163-2284-8 (hard cover)
    ISBN 10: 0-8163-2284-8
        1. Sermon on the mount. I. White, Ellen Gould Harmon, 1827–1915.
Thoughts from the Mount of Blessing. II. Title.

    BT380.3.T46 2009
    226.9'06—dc22

                                                                2008028892

08 09 10 11 12 • 5 4 3 2 1

DEDICATION

To

Max A. Trevino

and the

Southwestern Union Committee

for believing it should happen

CONTENTS

Introduction 7

1. On the Hillside by the Lake 11

2. Blessed (The Beatitudes) 16

3. What Keeping the Law Really Means.................... 47

4. The Real Reason to Help Others............................ 77

5. "Our Father"... 98

6. True Christianity 116

INTRODUCTION

ne day on a hillside, Jesus spoke to His disciples and to a vast crowd gathered with them. His words, which we call the "Sermon on the Mount," are heaven's blessing on our world. They are a gift to humanity, delivered as if spoken from the throne of heaven itself. Jesus, the Prince of preachers, the Master Teacher, spoke the words His Father gave Him.

These words give us a glimpse into what the kingdom of heaven is like. They show us the path we must walk to become like Jesus. They give us hope and sympathy during times of pain and sadness. They show us the way to find joy and peace as our lives unfold.

Seeming to forget that He was on this earth and not in heaven, Jesus greets the crowd with words that are commonly spoken in the realms of glory. He speaks words of blessing, which we call the "Beatitudes," not just to those who heard Him that morning, not just to those who believe in Him, but to the whole human family.

His words make clear what identifies a true follower of His. He leaves no doubt as to which character traits receive heaven's blessing. Turning away from the so-called elite, He speaks to the common people, the people the elite despised. Jesus offers these same blessings to everyone who chooses to follow Him. To the spiritually helpless, the gentle-hearted, the sad, the ostracized, the hated, and the abused, Jesus throws open His arms and says, "Come to Me, and I will give you peace."

In spite of the misery in this world, Jesus isn't at all sorry that He created human beings. With His infinite wisdom and love, He sees past the sin and sorrow to human possibilities—what we might achieve and become. In spite of how human beings have ignored God's mercy and destroyed their God-given dignity, the Creator will still be glorified when they are redeemed.

The words that Jesus spoke that day will never lose their power. Every sentence is a jewel of truth. The principles He expressed are for people of all ages and all walks of life. With hopeful faith in humanity, Jesus pointed out the character traits that bring us happiness and blessings. Through faith in Him, we can live up to those high standards and have the blessings He promised.

CHAPTER 1

ON THE HILLSIDE
BY THE LAKE

There was a mountain of blessing in the Old Testament. More than fourteen centuries before Jesus was born in Bethlehem, the Israelites gathered in the Shechem valley. From the mountains on either side, priests called out blessings and curses: "You will be blessed if you obey the commands of the LORD your God. . . . But you will be cursed if you disobey" (Deuteronomy 11:27, 28). The mountain where blessings were spoken became known as the "mount of blessing."

But the Israelites lost out on those blessings when they didn't follow God faithfully. Finally, God sent His own Son as Messenger to His people. On an unnamed hill beside the Sea of Galilee, Jesus spoke new words of blessing to His followers and to the vast crowds who drank in His message.

If we could sit there on the grassy hillside that day, listening alongside the disciples, we would hear Jesus' words as they understood them. If we try to place ourselves there today—try to put ourselves in that setting—we will find both hope and help there. And we will grasp a better understanding of what it means to be a follower of Jesus.

As Jesus began His ministry, the people of Israel were expecting the Messiah. But lost in traditions and ceremonies, they explained prophecies to agree with their pride and selfishness. So, they looked for the Messiah, not as a Savior from sin, but as a great political and military leader, who would avenge their nation and conquer the world.

If we could sit there on the grassy hillside that day, listening alongside the disciples, we would hear Jesus' words as they understood them.

John the Baptist, speaking like the prophets of old, called on them to repent, to give up their selfish hopes and dreams, and open their hearts to God. Right before their eyes, John pointed to Jesus and called Him the Lamb of God who had come to rid the world of sin. God was trying to remind them of Isaiah's prophecy of a Messiah who would suffer to save them. But they would not listen.

If the teachers and leaders in Israel had listened and let go of their selfish plans, if they had followed Jesus, He would have sent them out as His ambassadors to the world. John the Baptist had preached first to these leaders, announcing God's kingdom and calling for repentance. In driving out those who defiled the temple, Jesus announced to those same leaders that He was the Messiah, sent to cleanse the souls of His people and make their hearts a holy temple where God would live.

But the Jewish leaders were too proud to listen to a nobody

from Nazareth. When Jesus visited Jerusalem a second time, He was arrested and taken before the highest Jewish court. Only their fear of the crowds who followed Jesus everywhere kept the religious leaders from trying to have Him killed. After that, Jesus left Jerusalem and began His ministry in Galilee.

Jesus worked in Galilee several months, teaching and healing. The message went out to everyone who would listen: "The kingdom of heaven is near" (Matthew 4:17). This caught people's attention, fanning the flames of their national pride. The fame of this new Teacher spread beyond the boundaries of Galilee, and in spite of the attitude of the Jewish leaders, the feeling was widespread that He might be the hoped-for Deliverer. With feverish excitement, great crowds followed Jesus everywhere He went.

Now it was time for His closest disciples to join in His work, helping to care for the large crowds who followed Jesus. Some of the disciples had been with Jesus since the beginning of His ministry, and nearly all twelve had traveled and lived with Him like members of a family. But they had also been misled by the teachings of the rabbis so that, like the crowds, they expected Jesus to establish Himself soon as king of Israel. With this expectation, they couldn't understand what Jesus was doing. Why didn't He seek the support of the priests and rabbis? Why was He doing nothing to establish His authority as King?

These disciples had much to learn before Jesus could leave

Jesus worked in Galilee several months, teaching and healing. The message went out to everyone who would listen: "The kingdom of heaven is near."

them with the responsibility for His church on earth. But they had responded to Jesus' love, and He saw that He could train and teach them even though they were slow to see the truth of

Now it was time to teach them all the principles of His kingdom.

God's kingdom. They had been with Him long enough to begin to believe that He was on a divine mission from God. Many of the huge crowds that followed Jesus had seen much of His power. Now it was time to teach them all the principles of His kingdom.

Alone on a hilltop near the Sea of Galilee, Jesus spent all night in prayer for His chosen disciples. At dawn, He called them together and shared important lessons with them. He prayed with them and laid His hands on their heads and blessed them, dedicating them to the gospel work. Then He led them to the edge of the lake, where even at that early morning hour, a massive crowd was already gathering.

The disciples stayed close to their Master, feeling that something unusual was about to happen.

Besides the usual throngs of people from the towns in Galilee, a great many others had gathered as well—from Judea, Jerusalem, and half-pagan Decapolis; from far to the south and from Tyre and Sidon, the Phoenician cities on the shore of the Mediterranean. "They all came to hear Jesus teach and to be healed of their sicknesses" (Luke 6:18).

There wasn't enough room on the narrow lakeshore for everyone who wanted to hear Jesus, so He led them back to the hillside. At a level spot where there was room for everyone, Jesus sat down on the grass. His disciples and the crowd of people did the same.

The disciples stayed close to their Master, feeling that something unusual was about to happen. Jesus' actions earlier that morning made them think that He was going to announce His plans to become King. The people felt the excitement as well, and each person waited eagerly for Jesus' words. As they sat on the green hillside, they were filled with thoughts of their nation's future glory and power. Among them were scribes and Pharisees who looked forward to the day when they would rule over the hated Romans and claim the riches of the world's great empire. The peasants and fishermen hoped to hear that their poor houses and days of hard work, worry, and hunger would soon be replaced with mansions and days of ease. They hoped to trade in the simple garment they wore as a coat by day and used as a blanket by night for the rich robes of the Romans.

The heart of each person was filled with pride that Israel would soon be honored worldwide as God's chosen nation and that Jerusalem would be the capitol of the world.

CHAPTER 2

BLESSED (THE BEATITUDES)

*And he began to teach them: "Blessed are those who recognize they
are spiritually helpless. The kingdom of heaven belongs to them"
(Matthew 5:2, 3, God's Word).*

*J*esus didn't try to flatter the people or feed their
national pride. They had never heard such words
from a priest or rabbi. But the ideas presented by this
new Teacher held them spellbound. The sweetness of
divine love flowed out from Him like fragrance from a
flower. *Here is Someone who can read the secrets of my soul,* each listener thought, *but I can tell that He cares for me.* With open hearts
they listened, and the Holy Spirit helped them begin to understand what men and women have always needed to learn.

In those days, the religious leaders were sure of their spiritual
superiority. The Pharisee's prayer, "God, I thank you that I am
not like other people" (Luke 18:11), summed up their attitude—
and to a large extent, reflected the attitude of the whole nation.
But some in the crowd listening to Jesus that day had a sense of
their spiritual need.

When Peter saw Jesus' divine power at the miraculous catch

of fish, he fell at Jesus' feet, crying, "Go away from me, Lord. I am a sinful man!" (Luke 5:8). Like Peter, on that day many in the crowd felt "miserable, pitiful, poor, blind, and naked" (Revelation 3:17) in Jesus' presence. His opening words gave them hope.

Jesus had offered these same blessings to the country's leaders, but since they felt righteous and worthy, they turned away. Anyone who feels content with his spiritual condition, who feels worthy of salvation, won't see the need for Jesus' gift of grace and righteousness. A heart filled with pride has no room for Jesus and the blessings He can give. Such people are full of themselves, so they go away empty.

Those who know that they can't save themselves or do any good thing by their own power are the ones who appreciate what Jesus offers. They are the ones who have great spiritual needs. They are the ones Jesus declares to be blessed.

Jesus forgives, but through the Holy Spirit, He also leads us to feel sorrow for our sins and to ask for forgiveness. The Spirit leads us to see that we have nothing good in ourselves and that even the good we have done is mingled with selfishness and sin. Like the poor tax collector, we stand off with our eyes looking down and say, " 'God, have mercy on me, a sinner' " (Luke 18:13). Because we acknowledge our need, we are blessed and our sins are forgiven. God's promise is "Though your sins are like scarlet, they can be as white as snow. Though your sins are deep red, they can be white like wool" (Isaiah 1:18). And beyond just forgiving us, God also promises to give us a new heart.

Jesus didn't promise the spiritually needy an earthly kingdom, but a spiritual kingdom of His love, His grace, and His righteousness. As subjects of His kingdom, we are being changed—we are becoming like Him and ready "to have a share in all that he has prepared for his people in the kingdom of light" (Colossians 1:12).

If you sense something missing in your own soul, if you feel that you have nothing good inside, you can find goodness and strength in Jesus. You're not worthy of God's love, but Jesus *is* worthy, and He will save everyone who comes to Him. Whatever is in your past, however discouraging things may be at this moment, you can come to Jesus. You can come to Him just as you are—weak-willed, guilty, and depressed—and He will meet you with open arms. He will place His robe of righteousness around you and present you to His Father saying, "I have taken this sinner's place. Don't look at his life, but at Mine." Although Satan may claim us as his, Jesus' claim and power is stronger.

A SPECIAL PLACE IN GOD'S HEART

"Blessed are those who mourn. They will be comforted"
(Matthew 5:4, God's Word).

In this blessing, Jesus is referring to the genuine, heartfelt sadness that sin causes. When we picture Jesus on the cross, we can clearly see our human sinfulness, for it is sin that put Him there. We can see that even though God loves us with great tenderness, we often show no gratitude, ignoring Heaven's most precious Gift—our Friend Jesus. By ignoring Him, we've caused Him to suffer again the pain He felt at the cross. It's as if we're separated from God by a deep, dark chasm of sin, and it breaks our hearts.

But God comforts us in this sadness. He shows us our sin so we will run to Jesus and rejoice in the freedom He offers. When we are truly sorry and ready to be free of our sin, we can leave our burden of guilt at the cross.

Jesus' words also speak to those who are hurting or mourning because of grief. God doesn't cause these tragedies to happen (Lamentations 3:33), but He allows them so that we can grow closer to Him and learn to depend more on His strength (Hebrews 12:10). If we hold on to our faith during these difficult times, the trials that come will prove to be a blessing. The terrible blows that diminish our joy on earth can turn our eyes to heaven. Many would never have found Jesus if pain and sorrow hadn't led them to search for Him!

God uses the difficulties in our lives to chisel, square, and polish our rough edges, making our characters more like Jesus. This process can be painful—it hurts to be smoothed and polished by a sander! But God is carefully preparing those who trust Him to take their place in His heavenly temple.

It is a comfort to know that our Father in heaven never forgets those who have felt grief and sorrow. When King David fled from a rebellion led by his own son, he wept. Brokenhearted, David confessed his failure to God, and God didn't turn away from him. In fact, David was never closer to God's heart than during this difficult time.

The Lord says, "I correct and punish those whom I love. So be eager to do right, and change your hearts and lives" (Revelation 3:19). Jesus changes the hearts of those who, like David, recognize their sin and failure and their dependence on Him. He makes those hearts His home. But too many of us are like Jacob, who fought blindly against the very One who wanted to bless and save him. Like Jacob, we can find the peace we are looking for if we will learn to trust God even when He allows difficult times and uses them for our benefit.

"The one whom God corrects is happy, so do not hate being corrected by the Almighty. God hurts, but he also bandages up; he injures, but his hands also heal" (Job 5:17, 18). Jesus offers His healing love to each person who is sick or injured. Those whose lives are plagued by grief, pain, and loss can choose to feel Jesus' presence in their suffering.

God doesn't want us to remain beaten down by sorrowful, breaking hearts. We can look up and see the love on His face. Many whose eyes are blinded by tears fail to see that Jesus is standing right beside them. He wants so much for us to reach out with a simple faith that will let Him guide us. His heart is touched by our sorrow and our troubles. His everlasting love surrounds us, and we can meditate on that love all through the day. He will lift us above our troubles to a world of peace. Faith allows us to deal with our sorrow and to find joy and hope again.

This blessing is also promised to those who join Jesus in weeping for the pain and sin in the world. Jesus suffered great anguish on His path to save the world. The sin and selfishness around Him bruised His spirit. He worked so hard and suffered so much—only to see too many turn away from His offer of salvation. Each person who follows Him will feel some of this same pain. As we discover His love, we will join in His mission to save the lost. As we share in Jesus' sorrow and His mission, we will also share in His joy and glory.

Because Jesus suffered as a human, He knows how to console us when we are in pain. Because He was tempted to sin, He can save us when we are tempted. Because Jesus has saved us, we can minister to those around us who fall into sin and experience pain.

God has a special place in His heart for those who mourn, for He knows that sadness can melt hearts and help to save souls. His love opens a channel into our wounded souls and offers hope and healing to everyone who sorrows. "Praise be to the God and Father of our Lord Jesus Christ. God is the Father who is full of mercy and all comfort. He comforts us every time we have trouble, so when others have trouble, we can comfort them with the same comfort God gives us" (2 Corinthians 1:3, 4).

GENTLE LIKE JESUS

"Blessed are those who are gentle. They will inherit the earth"
(Matthew 5:5, God's Word).

This part of Jesus' sermon—the Beatitudes—shows us the path of a growing Christian. First, we recognize our spiritual need. Then we find that sin brings sadness, but that this sadness can be a blessing because it shows us our need for Jesus. Next, we learn about being gentle or meek.

Patience and meekness—the ability to respond gently even when we are wronged—were not character traits appreciated by the Jews of Jesus' day or by the other nations on earth. Under the inspiration of the Holy Spirit, Moses claimed to be the meekest man on earth, but that didn't strike the people of his day as a good thing. Instead, they viewed meekness with pity or a sneer. But Jesus listed gentleness as one of the most important qualifications for His kingdom—and showed gentleness in His own life.

Jesus was the Divine Ruler of heaven, but He gave it up and became a humble, created human—a servant. He walked among human beings not as a king demanding honor, but as a servant

on a mission. He didn't act as if He were better or more important than any other person. The Savior of the world was superior
to angels, but the humble way He lived and interacted with people made Him Someone they wanted to be around.

Jesus gave up His own interests and His own plans. Nothing
that He did on earth was for Himself. He lived only to do His
Father's will. When His mission on earth was almost over, Jesus
could say to His Father, "Having finished the work you gave me
to do, I brought you glory on earth" (John 17:4).

Jesus says to us, "Accept my teachings and learn from me, because I am gentle and humble in spirit" (Matthew 11:29). If we
are going to follow Jesus, we must give up on self and selfishness.
Like Jesus, we must live only to do our heavenly Father's will.

When we witness Jesus' selflessness, His humility, we see that
our self-sufficient independence comes from following Satan. It
is human nature to clamor for attention, but as we follow Jesus,
we learn to let go of our pride, our focus on ourselves, and, our
need to be in charge. No longer anxious to elbow our way to the
top, we find that our highest place is at the feet of our Savior. We
look to Jesus, waiting for His hand to lead us, listening for His
voice to guide us. The apostle Paul had this experience. He tells
us, "I was put to death on the cross with Christ, and I do not live
anymore—it is Christ who lives in me. I still live in my body, but
I live by faith in the Son of God who loved me and gave himself
to save me" (Galatians 2:20).

Jesus' presence in our lives gives us an abiding sense of peace.
Even though He was often surrounded by conflict, Jesus lived at
peace. No storm of human or satanic anger could disturb the
calm of His connection to God. To us He says, "I leave you peace;
my peace I give you. I do not give it to you as the world does. So

don't let your hearts be troubled or afraid" (John 14:27).

It is our own self-pride that destroys our peace. As long as we hold on to it, we need to defend ourselves from embarrassment and insults. But when we give it up, we pay no attention if we are ignored or insulted. Instead, we respond with love. "Love is patient and kind. Love is not jealous, it does not brag, and it is not proud. Love is not rude, is not selfish, and does not get upset with others. Love does not count up wrongs that have been done. Love is not happy with evil but is happy with the truth. Love patiently accepts all things. It always trusts, always hopes, and always remains strong. Love never ends" (1 Corinthians 13:4–8).

When happiness is based on earthly circumstances and relationships, it comes and goes. But the peace Jesus brings is constant. It doesn't depend on wealth, possessions, or friends. Peace flows from Jesus like a fountain, and that fountain never goes dry.

When our homes are filled with the gentle peace of Jesus, we have no reason to fight or argue angrily. Instead, this gentleness eases the stress and pressures of the day and soothes all those within the family circle. Wherever gentleness is cherished, it links the family on earth with the great family of heaven.

It's far better to live with being falsely accused than to retaliate against those who accuse us. The spirit of hatred and revenge began with Satan, and it brings only evil to those who harbor it. Gentleness and meekness come from Jesus and bring with them happiness and peace.

Those who are gentle and meek will inherit the earth. Sin entered this world because of selfishness, because of a desire for glory and importance. Through self-denial—through humility—Jesus saved this lost world from sin. If we, like Jesus, surrender our love of self and embrace gentleness, we will inherit the earth with Him.

And that earth will not be darkened with the shadow of death and the curse of sin. "God made a promise to us, and we are waiting for a new heaven and a new earth where goodness lives" (2 Peter 3:13). On that new earth, there will be no disappointment, no sadness, and no sin. No one will ever say, "I am sick," or "My loved one is dead." There will be no death, no funerals, no painful goodbyes, and no broken hearts. Jesus will be there, and there will be true peace.

WANTING TO BE CHANGED

"Blessed are those who hunger and thirst for righteousness, for they will be filled" (Matthew 5:6, NIV).

Righteousness is holiness, being like God. Righteousness is love, and love is the light and the life of God. Righteousness is living according to God's laws of love.

Jesus is the human picture of God's righteousness. He is righteous—right with God—and we become righteous also when we accept Him.

We can't earn rightness with God by hard work or painful struggle. We can't purchase it with a gift or by making a sacrifice. God freely gives His righteousness to every person who desires it as much as he or she desires food or water. "The LORD says, 'All you who are thirsty, come and drink. Those of you who do not have money, come, buy and eat! Come buy . . . without money and without cost' " (Isaiah 55:1).

Nothing humans can offer will satisfy this hunger and thirst of the soul. No one can meet this need except Jesus. He says, "Here

I am! I stand at the door and knock. If you hear my voice and open the door, I will come in and eat with you, and you will eat with me" (Revelation 3:20). He also says, "I am the bread that gives life. Whoever comes to me will never be hungry, and whoever believes in me will never be thirsty" (John 6:35).

Just as we need food to maintain our physical strength, we also need Jesus in order to maintain our spiritual life. He gives us strength to live with love like He did. We must depend on Him as much as we depend on food and water to keep us alive. Like a weary desert traveler needs to find a spring of cool water, we need Jesus.

The more we learn about our Savior's perfect character, the more we will want to become like Him. As we come to know God better, our understanding of His character will grow, and we will want to absorb His beauty and feel His power in our own lives. We will want most earnestly to be changed and become like Him. As we reach out to Him, God puts in our hearts a desire for His approval, a desire for righteousness.

If you feel this need in your own heart, if you are hungry and thirsty for God's approval, this means that Jesus is speaking to you. It means that He is working in your life to do for you the things that you cannot do for yourself, to give you things you cannot find for yourself.

How can we know what Jesus wants from us? We can find those answers in the Bible, the Word of God. His words in the Bible are like springs of water, and drinking from them will bring us face to face with Jesus. As we begin to absorb His Word, certain verses and stories will light up with new meaning, and we will understand truth in new ways and see clearly how these truths relate to our salvation. We will know that Jesus is satisfying our hunger to know Him better.

As the Holy Spirit helps us understand the Bible, we will be able to remember its truths and we will want to share them with others. Fresh, reassuring thoughts about the love of Jesus and His work in us will bubble up like water from a spring whenever we speak to others, whether or not they are fellow believers.

The Bible says, "Give, and it will be given to you" (Luke 6:38, NIV), because God's blessings are like a fountain of water. When we drink from this fountain of love, we find ourselves wanting more. And as we share our growing understanding of Jesus' love, we understand it more and feel it more deeply. The more we know about God, the more we will be able to know and the more we can share His love with others. "With God's power working in us, God can do much, much more than anything we can ask or imagine" (Ephesians 3:20).

Like showers of rain that refresh the earth, God pours out His love to everyone on earth through the Holy Spirit.

When Jesus left behind His life in heaven in order to come to our world and save us, He was given the unlimited help of the Holy Spirit. Each of Jesus' followers can have the same help if they will invite the Spirit to live in their hearts. God's command that we be filled with the Spirit is also a promise that we *will* be Spirit-filled if we surrender ourselves to Him.

Like showers of rain that refresh the earth, God pours out His love to everyone on earth through the Holy Spirit.

DEDICATED TO HELPING OTHERS

"Blessed are those who show mercy. They will be treated mercifully"
(Matthew 5:7, God's Word).

The human heart is naturally cold and selfish. Whenever someone shows kindness or mercy, it is because of the Holy Spirit's influence whether or not that person realizes it. God Himself is the Source of all mercy. He doesn't treat us as we deserve to be treated; He doesn't ask if we deserve to be loved. He just loves us, and that love gives us value and self-worth.

God isn't spiteful or mean. He isn't trying to punish us—He's trying to save us. Even when He permits difficult or painful events to happen to us, He works through these things to lead us to Him and to salvation. He wants so much to relieve our suffering, to give us comfort and peace. God never excuses the guilty, but He does want to take away their guilt.

When we show mercy, we share a bit of God's nature, and His love shines through us to others. When our hearts are connected to His heart of infinite love, we will also want to help people, not condemn them. Care and concern for others will continually flow out of our hearts if Jesus lives therein. Like Jesus, when we find others trapped and damaged by their own lifestyle choices, we won't ask, "Are they worth helping?" Instead, we'll ask, "How can I help them?" Even in the faces of the most depraved, most disgusting individuals, we will see only children of God in need of His love and saving grace.

Showing mercy means helping the poor, the sick and injured, and those who are trapped, addicted, or overburdened. The Bible describes it like this: "I saved the poor who called out and the orphan who had no one to help. The dying person blessed me, and I made the widow's heart sing. I put on right living as if it were clothing; I wore fairness like a robe and a turban. I was eyes for the blind and feet for the lame. I was like a father to needy

When our hearts are connected to His heart of infinite love, we will also want to help people, not condemn them.

people, and I took the side of strangers who were in trouble" (Job 29:12–16).

Many people struggle their way through life in misery, certain that they are worthless and hopeless. To someone who is struggling and lonely, a kind word, a sympathetic look, a sincere "thank you," would be as welcome as a cup of cold water to someone dying of thirst. And every act of unselfish kindness expresses Jesus' love for lost humanity.

There is a reward for those who show compassion for others. It comes in the peace and satisfaction of a life spent helping others. As the Bible teaches, we reap what we sow. "Happy is the person who thinks about the poor. When trouble comes, the LORD will save him. The LORD will protect him and spare his life and will bless him in the land. He will not let his enemies take him. The LORD will give him strength when he is sick, and he will make him well again" (Psalm 41:1–3).

If we dedicate our lives to helping others, we are linking ourselves to the God who holds the control of the universe in His hands. Our lives are tied to God with a golden chain of unbreakable promises—promises that will not be forgotten in our hour of need. The Bible says, "My God will use his wonderful riches in Christ Jesus to give you everything you need" (Philippians 4:19).

And when our lives finally come to an end, we will find a Savior of mercy eager to bring us one day to live with Him forever.

SEEING GOD CLEARLY

"Blessed are those whose thoughts are pure. They will see God"
(Matthew 5:8, God's Word).

The Jews of Jesus' day were so particular about ceremonial purity—their rituals for being considered holy or clean—that their rules turned every day into a heavy burden. They were so focused on the rules and laws, so afraid that they might be dirtied by some unholy or unclean thing or person that they didn't see the ugly stain that their selfishness and hate was leaving on their souls.

Our lives are tied to God with a golden chain of unbreakable promises— promises that will not be forgotten in our hour of need.

Jesus never suggested that being "ceremonially pure" was a requirement for being in His kingdom. But He did point out the need for a pure heart. "The wisdom that comes from God is first of all pure" (James 3:17). Everything in heaven will be pure and beautiful and clean, and those who live there will have pure hearts. As we learn more about Jesus, we will find that rudeness, crude language, and dirty thoughts make us uncomfortable and unhappy. When He lives in our hearts, there will be no room for cruel or offensive thoughts or actions.

But when Jesus said, "Blessed are those whose hearts are pure,"

He meant more than just "pure" in terms of not holding on to lust or careless sexuality. He meant having a heart that is not filled with pride but is also unselfish and trusting.

God is defined by self-sacrificing love. Unless we choose to live by the same selfless principle, we cannot know God. The natural human heart—deceived by Satan—sees God as a controlling dictator, enforcing His will on all. The selfish, power-hungry traits we see in humans—in ourselves—we insist on seeing in God, who says, "You thought I was just like you" (Psalm 50:21). We see His gifts and blessings as evidence that He wants only to punish and control us. In the same way, we see no value in the encouragement and direction found in the Bible.

To most of humanity, Jesus holds no attraction. They see nothing in Him that they want. When He was here on earth, the teachers and Pharisees told Him, "We say you are a Samaritan and have a demon in you" (John 8:48). Even His disciples were so blinded by their selfish hearts that it took them a long time to understand that He had come to show them His Father's love. That's why Jesus walked alone even when He was in a crowd. No one outside of heaven understood Him or His purpose.

When Jesus comes again in all His glory, those with impure hearts who have held on to their wicked ways will not be able to look at Him. The light of His presence will give eternal life to those who love Him, but will be the instrument of death for those who chose to reject Him; they will beg for a way to hide from the face of the One who died to save them.

But when our hearts are purified by the Holy Spirit, whom we have invited to live in us, everything changes. Now we can know God and understand His purposes. Just as Moses was hidden in the crevice of the mountain when God showed His glory to him, so we who are hidden in Jesus can see God's love.

"Whoever loves pure thoughts and kind words will have even the king as a friend," says Proverbs 22:11. By faith, we can see the Father here and now. We can see His kindness as He guides our way. We see Him in Jesus' character. The Holy Spirit helps us to understand the truth about God and about Jesus who He sent. As we grow in purity, we will see God in a new way—as a Redeemer. We will see what He is really like, the kind of love He has for us, and the loveliness of His character. We will see Him as a Father longing to hug a child who was lost and has returned home. These revelations will fill us with joy, and we will want nothing more than to reflect God's love to others.

With pure hearts, we will be able to see the hand of the Creator behind the mysteries and beauty of the universe. The words of Scripture that talk about His kindness, His mercy, and His love will be easier to understand and appreciate. The truths that the wisest scholars cannot understand will be clear to even the youngest Christians. The unique beauty of truth, which the worldly minded cannot understand, will become clearer and clearer to those who want nothing more than to know God's will and live by it. We grasp truth by becoming part of it, by absorbing God's nature and becoming like Him.

With pure hearts, we can live in the presence of God today and every day of our lives in this world. And we can also see Him face to face in the future, when we will be able to walk and talk with Him like Adam did. "Now we see but a poor reflection as in a mirror; then we shall see face to face" (1 Corinthians 13:12, NIV).

PEACE

"Blessed are those who make peace. They will be called God's children"
(Matthew 5:9, God's Word).

One of Jesus' titles is "the Prince of Peace." His mission is to bring peace back to earth and heaven. Sin destroyed that peace, but anyone who rejects sin and opens their heart to Jesus will share in the peace He brings.

True followers of Jesus will share His message of peace with the world.

Jesus is the only Source of true peace. His presence in our hearts eases our pain and quiets our anger. A person who is at peace with God and with those around him cannot be made miserable. There will be no room in such a person's heart for envy or hatred or evil thoughts. The peace of God within the heart will spread its calming influence like refreshing dew to everyone around him.

True followers of Jesus will share His message of peace with the world. Anyone who leads another person to God by showing Jesus' love in the way they live—in the things they do and say—is a peacemaker.

The spirit of peace that fills Jesus' followers is clear evidence of His presence in their lives. The joy with which they live, the kindness they show to others, and the integrity of their actions demonstrate to the world that they are Christians, true children of God. It is clear that they follow Jesus. As the Bible says, "Everyone who loves has become God's child and knows God" (1 John 4:7).

DOING WHAT GOD WANTS

"Blessed are those who are persecuted for doing what God approves of. The kingdom of heaven belongs to them" (Matthew 5:10, God's Word).

Jesus doesn't promise His followers fame and fortune in this world. He doesn't promise them a trouble-free life. Instead, He offers them the privilege of walking the same path He did, a path that seeks no praise or reward, a path that earns criticism and rejection from the world.

When He came to save our lost world, Jesus was opposed by all the enemies of God and humanity. Evil men and evil angels formed a cruel partnership against Him. Even though every word

Everyone who is filled with the spirit of Jesus will be criticized and harassed.

He spoke and every action He took showed nothing but divine kindness, He was so different from those around Him that many people responded with hostility and anger. Because He allowed no excuse for acting on the cruel impulses of human nature, people fought against Him.

The same thing happens to everyone who tries to live like Jesus. There is a never-ending conflict between righteousness and sin, between love and hate, between truth and lies. Whenever a person shares the love of Jesus, resistance and criticism rise up to fight against it. Whenever someone shares with another an understanding of Jesus and His way, he or she is pulling that person away from following Satan. This makes Satan angry, and he tries to stop what is happening. Everyone who is filled with the spirit of Jesus will be criticized and harassed. The form of the harassment or persecution may change, but the spirit behind it has been the same since the days of Abel.

As we begin to follow God's way, we will find that those in power will be against us—just as the powerful were against Jesus in His day. So this persecution should bring us joy instead of grief, because it proves that we are following in the steps of our Savior.

God doesn't promise that we won't face trials. He promises something far better. He says, "My grace is enough for you. When you are weak, my power is made perfect in you" (2 Corinthians 12:9). If you do go through a "fiery furnace" experience for the cause of God, Jesus will be with you just as He was with the three faithful Hebrews in Babylon. When we love the Lord, we'll find a sense of joy in knowing that we are suffering with Him and for Him.

Lies can damage our reputation, but they cannot stain our character.

All through the centuries, Satan has persecuted God's people. They have been tortured and killed, but their faithfulness to God has given them victory. Satan could imprison them and take their lives, but he could not touch their spirit. They could look past the immediate pain and loss and say, "The sufferings we have now are nothing compared to the great glory that will be shown to us" (Romans 8:18).

In times of trouble and persecution, God's people reveal His character. Hated by God's enemies, they learn from Jesus' example. Walking in His footsteps, they follow Jesus through difficult and painful times. Through suffering and sorrow, they learn the painful price of sin and guilt, and they determine to leave it behind. Because they have suffered with Jesus, they will also celebrate with Him in glory.

Describing a vision of heaven, John said, "I saw what looked like a sea of glass mixed with fire. All of those who had won the victory over the beast and his idol and over the number of his name were standing by the sea of glass. They had harps that God had given them. They sang the song of Moses, the servant of God, and the song of the Lamb: 'You do great and wonderful things, Lord God Almighty. Everything the Lord does is right and true, King of the nations' " (Revelation 15:2, 3).

WHEN PEOPLE INSULT YOU

"Blessed are you when people insult you, persecute you, lie, and say all kinds of evil things about you because of me" (Matthew 5:11, God's Word).

Since the beginning, Satan has worked by deception. He has always tried to misrepresent God, and through his influence, he also misrepresents God's people today. No one was ever slandered more cruelly than was Jesus. He was insulted and mocked because He insisted on living solely by the principles of God's holy law. People hated Him for no reason. But still, He stood calmly before His enemies and declared that Christians can always expect criticism and hate. He showed His followers how to meet the hatred of the world and encouraged them to stand against it.

Lies can damage our reputation, but they cannot stain our character. As long as we do not choose to sin, no one—satanic or human—can stain our souls. A person whose heart is committed to God is no different when facing the most difficult and discouraging situation than he is when all is well and God seems to be smiling upon him. Our words may be twisted, our motives maligned, even our actions may be misinterpreted, but this makes no real difference because we have bigger issues at risk. "We set our eyes not on what we see but on what we cannot see. What we see will last only a short time, but what we cannot see will last forever" (2 Corinthians 4:18).

When things are misunderstood or misrepresented, Jesus knows the truth. No matter what is said about us, we can wait patiently and trust Him because the truth will someday come to light. And those who have stood honorably with God will be honored by Him before the redeemed and angels.

God wants truth to be discussed and examined even if it involves persecution and criticism to make that happen.

Jesus said, "People will insult you and hurt you. They will lie and say all kinds of evil things about you because you follow me. But when they do, you will be happy. Rejoice and be glad, because you have a great reward waiting for you in heaven. People did the same evil things to the prophets who lived before you" (Matthew 5:11, 12). Adam's own faithful son, Abel, was killed because he was righteous. Enoch walked with God, but the world did not approve of him. Noah was mocked as a fanatic and a doomsayer. "Some were laughed at and beaten. Others were put in chains and thrown into prison" (Hebrews 11:36).

God's messengers have always been insulted and persecuted, but as a result, knowledge about God has spread even wider. Every follower of Christ should step forward and carry out the same work, knowing that everything done against God's people will help spread truth, not hold it back. God wants truth to be discussed and examined even if it involves persecution and criticism to make that happen. Every controversy, every criticism, and every attempt to deny people spiritual freedom are part of God's plan to awaken sleeping minds.

The history of God's messengers shows how true this is. When the Jewish Sanhedrin stirred up the crowd to stone Stephen to death, the message of the gospel was not hindered. Reports of how the light of heaven shone on Stephen's face as he died and the memory of the compassion in his final prayer, went like arrows into the hearts of those who witnessed his death and also into the hearts of those who heard the story.

One of those arrows struck the heart of the Pharisee Saul, and he was transformed into a witness for Christ to Jews and Gentiles, even to kings. Long years later, Paul wrote from his prison cell in Rome: "It is true that some preach about Christ because they are jealous and ambitious. . . . Others preach about Christ for selfish and wrong reasons, wanting to make trouble for me in prison. But it doesn't matter. The important thing is that in every way, whether for right or wrong reasons, they are preaching about Christ" (Philippians 1:15–18).

Through Paul's imprisonment, the gospel was spread further, and people even within Caesar's palace became believers. The more Satan tries to destroy the seed of God's Word, the more firmly it is planted in human hearts. As Jesus' followers are cursed and imprisoned, His name is lifted up, and others become believers.

Those who witness for Christ through persecution and criticism will be rewarded in heaven. But there is also a reward in this life for all who follow God. To know God, to better understand His purposes and His plans, to grasp more of His love, and glimpse more of His power is a treasure beyond human understanding. "I pray that you and all God's holy people will have the power to understand the greatness of Christ's love—how wide and how long and how high and how deep that love is. Christ's love is greater than anyone can ever know, but I pray that you will be able to know that love. Then you can be filled with the fullness of God" (Ephesians 3:18, 19).

This was the joy that filled Paul's and Silas's hearts when they prayed and sang praises to God at midnight in a jail in Philippi. The light of Jesus' presence drove out the gloom and lifted them up. From his prison in Rome, Paul delighted to hear reports of the spreading gospel: "So I am happy," he wrote, "and I will continue to be happy" (Philippians 1:18). And his message to the church at Philippi echoed the words of Jesus by the lake: "Be full of joy in the Lord always. I will say again, be full of joy" (Philippians 4:4).

THE SALT OF THE EARTH

"You are the salt of the earth" (Matthew 5:13).

Throughout history, salt has been valuable because of its ability to preserve food and keep it from spoiling. When Jesus called His followers "salt," He was teaching them that they could change the world around them by sharing their soul-saving message. God chooses people, not just to make them a part of His family, but to reach out through them to the rest of the world with the message of salvation.

God didn't choose Abraham just to increase His circle of friends; He chose Abraham to be a channel of blessing to the people of the earth. In His last prayer with His disciples before His crucifixion, Jesus said, "For their sake, I am making myself ready to serve so that they can be ready for their service of the truth" (John 17:19). As Christians are changed through the truth, they will, in turn, change the world and save it from complete moral decay.

By penetrating food, salt preserves and changes it. In the same way, the gospel changes people through personal contact and friendship with God's followers. We must make friends with those we hope to help. They will respond to the gospel as individuals, not in mass groups.

The saltiness of salt represents the true power of the Christian—the love of Jesus in the heart and the righteousness of Jesus in the life. If Jesus' love lives in our hearts, it will flow out to others. As we make friends with people, their hearts will be warmed by the unselfish kindness we show them. All sincere believers radiate a life-enhancing energy that touches and strengthens the people around them, especially those they are trying to reach with the gospel. This power is not ours, but the power of the Holy Spirit that begins to change hearts and minds.

When Jesus called His followers "salt," He was teaching them that they could change the world around them by sharing their soul-saving message.

In comparing His followers to salt, Jesus added a solemn warning: "If the salt loses its salty taste, it cannot be made salty again. It is good for nothing, except to be thrown out and walked on" (Matthew 5:13). Salt was often dumped out on streets and paths when it was no longer salty and therefore useless. As the people listened to Jesus' words, they could see white salt glistening in nearby pathways. It was a clear symbol of the uselessness of the religion of the Pharisees and its effect on their society.

Flavorless salt represents anyone who turns his or her back on the power of God's grace and grows cold. Whatever such a person does, he or she strikes those around them as uncaring and un-Christian. It is to these people that Jesus says, "I know what you do, that you are not hot or cold. I wish that you were hot or cold! But because you are lukewarm—neither hot, nor cold—I am ready to spit you out of my mouth" (Revelation 3:15, 16).

If we don't have the grace and kindness of Jesus, we are testifying to the world around us that the truth we claim to believe has no reality, no power.

Without a living faith in Christ as a personal Savior, it is impossible to influence those around us in this skeptical world. We cannot give what we do not have. We can bless and uplift those around us only as much as we are blessed and lifted up by our own devotion and dedication to Christ. If we have no love, if we do nothing to help others, if we have no real Christian experience, then we have no power to help, no connection with heaven, no sense of Christ in our lives. Unless the Holy Spirit can communicate the truth of Jesus through us to the world, we are just like salt that has lost its saltiness. We're worthless.

If we don't have the grace and kindness of Jesus, we are testifying to the world around us that the truth we claim to believe has no reality, no power. As far as our influence goes, the Word of God means nothing.

I may speak in different languages of people or even angels. But if I do not have love, I am only a noisy bell or a crashing cymbal. I may have the gift of prophecy. I may understand all the secret things of God and have all knowledge, and I may have faith so great I can move mountains. But even with all these things, if I do not have love, then I am nothing. I may give away everything I have, and I may even give my body as an offering to be burned. But I gain nothing if I do not have love (1 Corinthians 13:1–3).

When love fills our hearts, it will become the ruler of our lives and will flow out unselfishly to others, not because of any favor they have done for us. Love changes a person, giving him control of his impulses, his anger, and his affections. This kind of love, like the love of the angels in heaven, is as wide as the universe. When it's cherished in our hearts, it will sweeten our entire lives and bless all those around us. It is this love—and only this love—that can make us the salt of the earth.

THE LIGHT OF THE WORLD

"You are the light that gives light to the world" (Matthew 5:14).

It was still morning when the people gathered by the lake to hear Jesus. As always, He kept their attention by using interesting examples from nature and the things they could see around them. On this particular day, the glorious sun was climbing higher and higher in the blue sky, chasing away the shadows that lurked in the valleys and the narrow mountain passes. As the sunlight flooded the land with its splendor, the calm surface of the lake reflected the golden light and mirrored the rosy clouds of morning. Every flower and leaf glistened with dew, and the birds sang sweetly among the trees. Nature smiled as a new day began.

Jesus looked out at the people before Him and then at the rising sun. He said to His disciples, "You are the light of the world" (NIV). Just like the sun rises each day to drive out the shadows and awaken the world to life, Christians are to go out sharing the light of heaven with those who are in darkness from error and sin.

In the brilliant light of the morning, the towns and villages on the surrounding hills stood out clearly. Pointing to them, Jesus said, "A city that is built on a hill cannot be hidden. And people don't hide a light under a bowl. They put it on a lampstand so the light shines for all the people in the house" (Matthew 5:14, 15).

Most of those who were listening to Jesus that morning were peasants and fishermen whose small homes had only one room. A single lamp on a stand gave light to the whole house. But Jesus encouraged them to shine for others. "In the same way, you should be a light for other people. Live so that they will see the good things you do and will praise your Father in heaven" (Matthew 5:16).

> *The only true light that has ever shone or will ever shine on human beings is the light that radiates from Jesus.*

The only true light that has ever shone or will ever shine on human beings is the light that radiates from Jesus. He is the only Light that can illuminate the darkness of a sinful world. Of Jesus the Bible says, "In him there was life, and that life was the light of all people" (John 1:4). By receiving His life, Jesus' disciples became light bearers also. With the example of Jesus' life in their hearts and His love showing in their characters, they became the light of the world.

In ourselves, we have no light. Apart from Christ, we are like an unlit candle, like the moon lying within the shadow of the earth. We don't have a single ray of light to shine into our dark world. But when we turn to Jesus, the Sun of Righteousness, when we come in touch with Him, our souls light up with His brightness.

God's blessings come from human hands.

Jesus' followers must be more than just a light to the people around them. They are *the* light of the world. Jesus says to everyone who believes in Him, "You have given yourselves to Me, and I am sending you to the world to represent Me." As Jesus was sent to represent the Father, so we are sent to represent Jesus. Our Savior is the Source of light, but don't forget that He shines into the world through human beings. God's blessings come from human hands. Jesus Himself came to our world as the Son of man. The church, made up of each individual disciple, is the channel heaven uses to reveal God to humanity. Angels are waiting to spread heaven's light and power through us to those in danger of being lost. And what if we fail to do our assigned work? Then, to that degree, the world loses the life-changing influence of the Holy Spirit it might have had.

He teaches us to see every person in need as a neighbor and to see the world as our neighborhood.

Jesus didn't say to the disciples, "Try to make your light shine." He said, "*Let* it shine." When Jesus lives in a person's heart, the light is impossible to hide. The light of His love will shine out.

When those who claim to be Christians don't shine with the light of God's love, it can be only because they have lost their connection to the Source of that light.

Throughout history, the Spirit of Christ has made God's true followers the light to the people of their day. Joseph was a light bearer in Egypt. With purity and kindness and brotherly love, he represented Christ in the middle of a culture that worshiped many gods. While the Israelites traveled from Egypt to Canaan, the faithful among them shone like a light, revealing God to the surrounding nations. From Daniel and his friends in Babylon, as well as from Mordecai in Persia, bright beams of light shone out, combating the darkness in the courts of kings.

Just as the rays of the sun reach the farthest edges of the earth, God wants the light of the gospel to reach every person in the world.

In the same way, Christ's disciples today must be light bearers. Through us, the Father's mercy and goodness are shown to a world darkened by a misunderstanding of God. By seeing our acts of love, others are led to God. Our lives make it clear that there is a praiseworthy God on the throne of the universe, One after whom we can pattern our lives. The glow of divine love in our hearts and the peace and harmony of Jesus in our lives are glimpses of heaven to those around us. This is the way people are led to believe that God loves them. This is how their sinful hearts are purified and transformed.

With the words, "You are the light of the world," Jesus committed His followers to a worldwide mission (NIV). In Jesus' day, selfishness, pride, and prejudice had built a wall between the Jews—

the guardians of God's truth—and the rest of the world. But Jesus came to change that. The words people heard from His lips were not like anything they had ever heard from the priests or rabbis. Jesus tore down that selfish wall of prejudice and taught that we should love everyone, everywhere. His love lifts people out of their small selfish circles and abolishes national and social distinctions. Jesus sees no difference between neighbors and strangers or friends and enemies. He teaches us to see every person in need as a neighbor and to see the world as our neighborhood.

Just as the rays of the sun reach the farthest edges of the earth, God wants the light of the gospel to reach every person in the world. If God's church was living up to His plan, the light would reach everyone who sits in darkness. Instead of meeting together each week in comfort and forgetting their mission, church members would scatter out into the nations, letting their light shine and carrying the gospel to the whole world.

This is the way that God's plan to gather followers has always been fulfilled—from Abraham on the plains of Mesopotamia to our day. God says, "I will bless you. . . . And you will be a blessing to others" (Genesis 12:2). If the glory of God has touched your heart, if you have seen the beauty of His love, then Jesus is speaking to you. Have you felt God's life-changing power? Then many others who are addicted to sin and sorrow are waiting to hear your words of faith.

We can't be satisfied just to know about God's love and power. We must share what we know with others. The prophet Isaiah and King David both saw the glorious love of God and then shared their response in poetry and song. Who can see Jesus' glory and His plan to save men and women—and not share it with others? Who could be touched by the incomprehensible love Jesus showed on the cross to save us—and not praise God to everyone who will listen?

The writer of the Psalms praised God with a song, saying, "Parents will tell their children what you have done. They will retell your mighty acts, wonderful majesty, and glory. And I will think about your miracles. They will tell about the amazing things you do, and I will tell how great you are" (Psalm 145:4–6).

Who could be touched by the incomprehensible love Jesus showed on the cross to save us—and not praise God to everyone who will listen?

Whenever the story of the Cross is told, it captures people's minds and focuses their thoughts. Then their spiritual senses are charged with divine power, and their energy can be concentrated on God's work. These workers will brighten the earth like beams of light.

Jesus gladly accepts the efforts of every person who follows Him. Through Him, humanity combines with the divinity, and the mysteries of God's gift of love are explained. We can talk about that love, pray about it, sing about it, and broadcast it all over the earth.

The light of God's love shines brightly in contrast to the dark and selfish heart. That light shines when we handle troubles patiently, when we receive blessings gratefully, when we resist temptation, when we show humility, kindness, mercy, and love every day in everything we do.

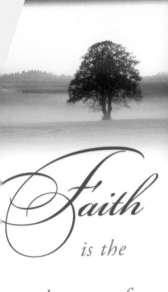

$\mathcal{F}$aith

is the

substance of

things hoped for,

the evidence of

things not seen.

Hebrews 11:1

U9110

© Warner Press, Inc
Made in USA

7 30817 33990 0

emphasized strongly enough the importance of keeping the law. When He explained the actual truths on which their rituals and rules were based, they accused Him of plotting to do away with God's law.

As Jesus spoke to the people on the mountainside about God's law, He spoke calmly, but with such power and conviction that their hearts were touched. They were accustomed to the rabbis lifelessly reciting rules, so Jesus' words shocked them. They "were amazed at his teaching, because he did not teach like their teachers of the law. He taught like a person who had authority" (Matthew 7:28, 29).

The Pharisees could see the difference in Jesus' teaching style also. And they could see that His explanation of the power and beauty of truth—so simple yet so deep—was captivating the people. They could see that His gentle, loving manner was opening the people's hearts. It was clear to them that Jesus' teaching was destroying everything they had taught and worked for. He was tearing down the walls that gave them their proud, exclusive status. They were afraid that if they didn't do something, Jesus would turn everyone completely against them. So they followed Him, watching for some way to discredit Him in front of the crowds and thus pave the way to have Him arrested and killed.

Everything in nature, from a dust particle caught in a sunbeam to the planets orbiting the sun, follows natural laws.

On this day by the sea, spies were closely watching Jesus as usual. While Jesus explained the true principles of righteousness, the followers of the Pharisees were whispering that His teaching went against the laws given at Mount Sinai. Of course, nothing Jesus said was out of harmony with the teachings of Moses. After all, everything Moses had taught the people came from Jesus! But the whispering caused many to think that Jesus had come to do away with the law. So Jesus made His position clear. He said, "Don't think that I have come to tear down the law of Moses or the teaching of the prophets" (Matthew 5:17).

This was the Creator speaking, the Giver of the law, who made it clear that He had no intention of setting the law aside. Everything in nature, from a dust particle caught in a sunbeam to the planets orbiting the sun, follows natural laws. The order and harmony of the universe depend on it. In the same way, there are natural laws of righteousness that apply to all intelligent beings, and the well-being of the universe depends on our following these laws as well.

Even before this earth existed, God's law was in place. Angels live by its principles, and if earth is going to be in harmony with heaven, so must human beings. Christ introduced humanity to this law at Creation, "while the morning stars sang together and all the angels shouted with joy" (Job 38:7). Jesus' mission on earth wasn't to destroy the law, but to enable us to obey it again.

Many years later, the beloved disciple John, who was listening to Jesus that day by the sea, wrote about our never-ending need to keep the law. He wrote, "The person who sins breaks God's law. Yes, sin is living against God's law" (1 John 3:4). John made it clear that he was "not writing a new command to you but an old command you have had from the beginning" (1 John 2:7). He was referring to the law that existed before Creation and that had been stated again at Mount Sinai.

Jesus said, "I have not come to abolish them [the law] but to fulfill them" (Matthew 5:17, NIV). By "fulfill," He meant to keep or measure up to the law's conditions, to perfectly obey God's will. His mission was to show the greatness and glory of the law (Isaiah 42:21), to show that it applies in all situations, and that it will do so forever.

As long as heaven and earth exist, the holy principles of God's law will remain.

Christ's holy, beautiful character had been praised by prophets and kings of ages past, and it was a living example of the character of God's law. Throughout His life on earth, Jesus showed that heavenly love lies just beneath the surface of each of the commandments. And He proclaimed that the law is eternal: "I tell you the truth, nothing will disappear from the law until heaven and earth are gone. Not even the smallest letter or the smallest part of a letter will be lost until everything has happened" (Matthew 5:18).

By obeying the law Himself, Christ showed not only that it must be followed but that through His grace and strength, every human being can obey it. On this day He made it clear that not one small thing about the law would change until the plan of salvation is complete. No, the law can never change, and as far as the human eye can see into the future, it will always have authority. As long as heaven and earth exist, the holy principles of God's law will remain. And God's righteousness will continue to bless the earth like streams of living water.

Because God's law is perfect and unchangeable, it is impossible for sinful human beings to obey it—in their own power. That is why Jesus came to this earth as our Savior. His mission was to connect humanity to divinity, to bring human beings back into harmony with the laws of heaven. When we turn our backs on sin and accept Jesus as our Savior, the law is honored. As Paul asks,

Whenever we choose to do things our own way, we are going against God's way.

"So do we destroy the law by following the way of faith? No! Faith causes us to be what the law truly wants" (Romans 3:31).

Jesus offers a new agreement, a new promise: "This is the agreement I will make with them at that time, says the Lord. I will put my teachings in their hearts and write them on their minds" (Hebrews 10:16). The Jewish system of symbols that pointed forward to Jesus as the sacrificial Lamb of God ended at His death, but the principles contained in the Ten Commandments are as unchangeable as the throne of heaven itself. Those principles were known and in place in the paradise of the Garden of Eden, and it will be the same in the paradise of heaven. When Eden blooms on earth again, God's law of love will be obeyed by everyone who lives under God's unending love.

OBEYING GOD'S LAWS

"Whoever refuses to obey any command and teaches other people not to obey that command will be the least important in the kingdom of heaven"
(Matthew 5:19).

People who do not live by any of the principles of God's kingdom will have no place there. We cannot break one commandment and keep all the others. "A person who follows all of God's law but fails to obey even one command is guilty of breaking all the commands in that law" (James 2:10). The significant thing is not the magnitude of the specific act of disobedience; what matters is that the act of disobedience itself shows that our hearts are not totally in harmony with God. It shows that there is still within us some element of rebellion against God's authority.

If we were free to set aside God's law and create our own standards of conduct, then "acceptable behavior" would vary wildly, ensuring that life would be neither fair nor kind. With the authority taken out of God's hands and with human selfishness in charge, God's desire to protect and save human beings would be ignored and disrespected.

Whenever we choose to do things our own way, we are going against God's way. We don't belong in heaven if we're fighting against the principles of God's kingdom. And when we go against God, we automatically join sides with Satan, the enemy of God and humanity. We must live by the words of God. We can't disregard any of God's words—any of His teachings or principles— and be safe. All of the commandments protect our happiness in this life, as well as in the eternal life to come. Obeying God's law surrounds us with a protective barrier and keeps us away from evil. If we break down this barrier, we open a way for Satan to create pain and loss in our lives.

By going against God's will in just one area, the first human pair brought death and pain to the whole world. And everyone who follows their example will add to it. God's love underlies every principle of His law, and anyone who breaks these principles is creating his or her own unhappiness and destruction.

A RELIGION BASED ON RULES

"I tell you that if you are no more obedient than the teachers of the law and the Pharisees, you will never enter the kingdom of heaven" (Matthew 5:20).

The Jewish leaders accused Jesus and His disciples of being sinners because they ignored the rituals and ceremonies of the rabbis. This confused the disciples. They were accustomed to listening to and honoring these religious leaders. But Jesus exposed their religion and self-righteousness as worthless. The Jewish nation claimed to be God's chosen people, but Jesus showed that their religion had no saving faith. All their attempts to appear righteous, all their rituals and ceremonies, all their claims of living without breaking God's law, did not make them holy. Their hearts were not pure; they were not kind and just; they were not like Jesus.

A religion based on keeping laws or rules doesn't bring a person into harmony with God. The Pharisees' hard, rigid belief system showed no

The only true religion is the one that works to change people's hearts with love.

kindness, forgiveness, or love; it was actually a barrier to sinners. It kept people away from God. Like salt that has lost its saltiness, the beliefs of the Jewish leaders did nothing to save the world from spoiling with sin. The only true religion is the one that works to change people's hearts with love. That kind of religion can transform a person's character.

The Jewish people should have learned all this from the teachings of the prophets. Hundreds of years earlier, the prophet Micah had addressed the same issue: "You say, 'What can I bring with me when I come before the LORD, when I bow before God on high? Should I come before him with burnt offerings, with year-old calves? Will the LORD be pleased with a thousand male sheep? Will he be pleased with ten thousand rivers of oil?' . . . The LORD has told you, human, what is good; he has told you what he wants from you: to do what is right to other people, love being kind to others, and live humbly, obeying your God" (Micah 6:6–8).

The prophet Hosea compared the Pharisees' type of religion to an empty vine that produces fruit only for itself. The righteousness of the Jewish leaders was the "fruit" of their own efforts to keep the law according to their own ideas and for their own selfish benefit. Clearly, their righteousness could be no better than they were themselves. In trying to make themselves holy, they were trying to make a "clean" thing out of an "unclean" thing. God's law is as holy and perfect as He is. It shows humans what God's righteousness is like. Human nature is twisted and selfish, so it's impossible for human beings, by their own power, to keep God's law. The actions of a selfish heart are dirty with sin and "all the right things we have done are like filthy pieces of cloth" (Isaiah 64:6).

The law is holy, but the Jews could not become holy by trying to keep it. So the followers of Jesus had to look for something different from what the Pharisees taught if they wanted to enter the kingdom of heaven. God gave them His Son, whose life was a perfect reflection of the law. If they would open their hearts and accept Jesus, then God would live in them and His love would transform them into someone like Him. God would give them the righteousness that the law demands. But the Pharisees rejected Jesus. They were intent on earning their own righteousness and would not stoop to learn about the righteousness of God.

Jesus showed those who listened to Him what it means to keep the commandments—it means reflecting His character in their own lives and actions.

A SPIRIT OF HATE

"But I tell you, if you are angry with a brother or sister, you will be judged"
(Matthew 5:22).

Jesus' words made it clear to His listeners that when they condemned others for sinning, their meanness and hate made them just as guilty as the ones they condemned.

Through the prophet Moses, God had said, " 'You must not hate your fellow citizen in your heart. . . . Forget about the wrong things people do to you, and do not try to get even. Love your neighbor as you love yourself' " (Leviticus 19:17, 18). Jesus' teachings had been taught by the prophets long before, but they had become hidden because of hard hearts and the love of sin. Jesus' words made it clear to His listeners that when they condemned others for sinning, their meanness and hate made them just as guilty as the ones they condemned.

Across the lake from the spot where Jesus was preaching that morning was the region called Bashan, a remote area of wild canyons and forests that was a favorite hiding place for criminals of all kinds. Everyone listening to Jesus had heard recent reports of robberies and murders committed there, and many were quick to condemn these evil people. But at the same time, they themselves were hotheaded and contrary. They felt bitter hatred for the Romans who ruled them, and they felt free to hate and despise anyone else, even other Jews who didn't do and believe everything the way they did. So they were clearly breaking the spirit of the commandment, "You must not murder anyone."

The spirit of hate and revenge started with Satan, and it led him to kill the Son of God. Anyone who enjoys cruelty or meanness is embracing the same spirit, and it will lead to pain and death. Just as a plant lies dormant within a seed, an evil act lies within every thought of revenge. "Everyone who hates a brother or sister is a murderer, and you know that no murderers have eternal life in them" (1 John 3:15).

"If you say bad things to a brother or sister, you will be judged by the council" (Matthew 5:22). By giving His own Son to save us, God shows how highly He values every human soul, and He gives no one permission to harshly criticize or insult another person.

> *God will hold us responsible for every cruel and critical word spoken about a person for whom Jesus gave His life.*

We may see the faults and weaknesses of those around us, but God considers each person to be His property—His, because He is their Creator, and doubly His, because He paid for their salvation with the blood of Christ. Every human being has been created in His image, and even the most pitiful ones should be treated with respect and kindness. God will hold us responsible for every cruel and critical word spoken about a person for whom Jesus gave His life. Besides, "Who says you are better than others? What do you have that was not given to you? And if it was given to you, why do you brag as if you did not receive it as a gift?" (1 Corinthians 4:7).

"And if you call someone a fool, you will be in danger of the fire of hell" (Matthew 5:22). In the Old Testament, the word *fool* is used to describe someone who has given up his faith and turned to a life of wickedness. Here Jesus says that anyone who condemns someone else as an enemy of God has earned the same condemnation.

When Jesus fought with Satan over the body of Moses, He did not accuse or condemn him. If He had, He would have stooped to Satan's own level, because accusation is one of Satan's weapons. Jesus said only, "The Lord punish you" (Jude 9).

It would be a sham to express faith in a God of love and forgiveness while holding on to anger or hate for someone.

Jesus sets this example for us. When we argue with or struggle against the enemies of Christ, we shouldn't speak in a spirit of retaliation or accuse them of anything. Someone who speaks for God shouldn't use words that Jesus Himself wouldn't use even against Satan. We must leave all the judging and condemning to God.

MAKING THINGS RIGHT

"Go and make peace with that person" (Matthew 5:24).

God's love is not a list of things to avoid doing. God's love is positive and active, a living spring of water always flowing to bless others. If that love lives in our hearts, we will do more than just not hate others; we will search for ways to show love and kindness to them.

Jesus said, "So when you offer your gift to God at the altar, and you remember that your brother or sister has something against you, leave your gift there at the altar. Go and make peace with that person, and then come and offer your gift" (Matthew 5:23, 24). The offerings the Jews brought to God expressed their faith that through the Messiah, they would receive mercy and love from God. But it would be a sham to express faith in a God of love and forgiveness while holding on to anger or hate for someone.

When someone who claims to follow God offends or hurts another person, he or she misrepresents God to that person. This must be made right by confessing it as sin. Even if the other person has done more to hurt us than we have done to them, we are still responsible for our part. When we come to God in prayer or to give an offering, if we remember something we have said or done to hurt another person, we should go at once to confess and ask forgiveness.

If we have done anything to cheat, trick, or financially injure someone, we should compensate him or her for the damage we have done. If we have misquoted someone or twisted his words to imply a different meaning or injured someone's reputation in any way, we should go to the ones we spoke to and retract our damaging words.

If disagreements between fellow believers were not made a public matter, but worked out between them in a spirit of Christian love, much evil and negative publicity could be prevented. If Jesus' followers were tied together by His love, the bitterness that afflicts so many could be erased.

IMAGINED IMMORALITY

"I tell you that if anyone looks at a woman and wants to sin sexually with her, in his mind he has already done that sin with the woman" (Matthew 5:28).

The Jewish people took pride in their morality. They were horrified by the immoral behavior of the people around them. The Roman officers stationed in Palestine were especially offensive because they brought their corrupt customs and lustful appetites with them. In Capernaum, these Roman bureaucrats haunted the gardens and public pathways with their giddy lovers.

It will take the ages of eternity to discover the destiny God has planned for His human children when they are remade in His image.

Often, the stillness of the lake was shattered by the sounds of partying and lusty laughter from their pleasure boats. The people expected Jesus to condemn this wicked behavior, but He shocked them by pointing to the impurity inside their own hearts.

When impure thoughts are cherished, even secretly, sin still controls the heart. The soul is still locked in bitterness and depravity. Many find pleasure in imagining scenes of immorality and enjoy evil thoughts and lustful looks. But the true nature of the evil they think hidden—the shame and heartbreaking grief—is clearly seen when similar actions are exposed publically. The temptation that leads a person to sin does not create the weakness or evil that is shown by the act of sin. Temptation merely exposes what was already being imagined in the heart. What we hide in our hearts shows who we really are.

SURRENDERING SELF

"If your right hand causes you to sin, cut it off and throw it away"
(Matthew 5:30).

Most people would agree to have their hand cut off if doing so would save their life. So shouldn't we be even more willing to cut off whatever is threatening our souls spiritually? The gospel reaches souls that are in slavery to Satan and saves them, giving them the glorious freedom of God's children. God's plan is not just to rescue us from the pain and suffering that sin always brings, but to save us from sin itself. Our souls, wicked and twisted as they are, will be transformed and purified, clothed in the beauty of God and changed to be like Jesus. "No one has ever seen this, and no one has ever heard about it. No one has ever imagined what God has prepared for those who love him" (1 Corinthians 2:9). It will take the ages of eternity to discover the destiny God has planned for His human children when they are remade in His image.

Like every other gift God has given to humanity, marriage has been distorted by sin.

If we are going to reach this high and holy standard, then we must eliminate anything that might cause us to stumble. Sin keeps its hold on us through the will. Here Jesus compares surrendering the will to plucking out an eye or cutting off a hand. Does it seem that surrendering your will to God might result in your going through life wounded or crippled? Even if it does, isn't it better to be wounded and crippled if by doing so you reach heaven? It may seem like a tragedy, but it is actually a great blessing.

God is the Source of life, and we have life only if we are connected to Him. We may be able to exist for a short time separated from God, but we don't really have life. The Bible says that she "who uses her life to please herself is really dead while she is alive" (1 Timothy 5:6). Only when we surrender our will to God can He give us life. Only by accepting His life can we overcome our hidden sins. We can bury them in our hearts and hide them from human eyes, but how can we stand before God with open hearts?

God's love and grace can bring together two estranged hearts and unite them together with bonds of love that can endure any trial or problem.

If we hold on to self and refuse to surrender our will to God, we are choosing death. God is a consuming fire to sin. So when His presence consumes sin, it will consume us also if we choose sin and refuse to separate ourselves from it.

It is a sacrifice to give ourselves to God. But it is a sacrifice of earthly things for spiritual things, of life that ends for a life that never ends. God doesn't want to destroy our will. We must use it to do the things He asks us to do. If we give our will to Him, He will return it to us, purified and strengthened and so closely tied to Him that He can pour out His love and power through us to the world. However difficult this surrender appears to be to, it is the best decision we can ever make.

In his battle with the Angel, Jacob didn't win until he gave up and surrendered. Then, after he was crippled and weak, Esau's armed men didn't fight him, and Pharaoh, the proud Egyptian ruler, knelt and asked for his blessing. In the same way, Jesus, the Captain of our salvation, won His battle with Satan by surrendering to His Father's will. Out of weakness, we can become strong and claim the victory of heaven.

THE BLESSING OF MARRIAGE

"Is it right for a man to divorce his wife for any reason he chooses?"
(Matthew 19:3).

Among the Jews in Jesus' day, a man was allowed to divorce his wife for the most trivial reasons, and the woman was then free to marry again. This practice created a great deal of misery and sin. In His sermon by the lake, Jesus plainly declared that a marriage should never end unless one of the two had been unfaithful. He said, "Anyone who divorces his wife forces her to be guilty of adultery. The only reason for a man to divorce his wife is if she has sexual relations with another man. And anyone who marries that divorced woman is guilty of adultery" (Matthew 5:32).

When the Pharisees later questioned Jesus about the legality of divorce, Jesus reminded them that marriage had been established at Creation. He said, "Moses allowed you to divorce your wives because you refused to accept God's teaching, but divorce was not allowed in the beginning" (Matthew 19:8). Marriage and the Sabbath both began in Eden, and both were given to bring glory to God and to help humanity. When God joined Adam and

Eve together in marriage, the Bible says, "So a man will leave his father and mother and be united with his wife, and the two will become one body" (Genesis 2:24). This established the law of marriage for all time, and God the Father pronounced it good.

Like every other gift God has given to humanity, marriage has been distorted by sin. But the gospel of Christ can restore its purity and beauty. In both the Old and New Testaments, marriage is used to illustrate the sacred relationship between Christ and His people. "Don't be afraid," He says. "The God who made you is like your husband. His name is the LORD All-Powerful. The Holy One of Israel is the one who saves you" (Isaiah 54:4, 5). In the Song of Solomon, we hear the bride—representing God's people—crying, "My lover is mine, and I am his" (Song of Solomon 2:16). And the response of the One who loves her is, "My darling, everything about you is beautiful, and there is nothing at all wrong with you" (Song of Solomon 4:7).

Everything we own comes stamped with a cross, bought with the most precious blood of all.

Later, the apostle Paul, writing to the believers at Ephesus, explained that God set the husband in place as the head of the family, to protect his wife and tie the family members together. In the same way, Jesus is the Head of the church and the Savior of its body of believers. He says,

> Wives, yield to your husbands, as you do to the Lord, because the husband is the head of the wife, as Christ is the head of the church. . . .
> Husbands, love your wives as Christ loved the church

and gave himself for it to make it belong to God. Christ used the word to make the church clean by washing it with water. He died so that he could give the church to himself like a bride in all her beauty. He died so that the church could be pure and without fault, with no evil or sin or any other wrong thing in it. In the same way, husbands should love their wives as they love their own bodies (Ephesians 5:22–28).

Only the grace of Christ can make marriage a blessing that elevates all humans the way God intended it to do. In this way, the families of earth, in their harmony, peace, and love, represent the family of heaven.

Everything that Christians do should be as transparent as the sunlight.

Just as it was in Jesus' day, the state of marriage today is a poor reflection of heaven's idea of what it should be. But for those who have found bitterness and disappointment in marriage, instead of the companionship and joy for which they had hoped, the gospel offers comfort and support. The presence of the Spirit is a calming influence, instilling gentle patience and hope. When the heart is filled with the love of Jesus, it will not be consumed with a desire to attract sympathy and attention. And when the soul is surrendered to God, His wisdom will do in us what our human wisdom cannot. God's love and grace can bring together two estranged hearts and unite them together with bonds of love that can endure any trial or problem.

SPEAK THE TRUTH, AND NOTHING BUT THE TRUTH

"Never swear an oath" (Matthew 5:34).

Jesus gives the reason we should not swear: "Don't swear an oath using the name of heaven, because heaven is God's throne. Don't swear an oath using the name of the earth, because the earth belongs to God. . . . Don't even swear by your own head, because you cannot make one hair on your head become white or black" (Matthew 5:34–36).

Everything comes from God. We don't have anything that He hasn't given us. Actually, we don't have anything that wasn't bought for us by the blood of Christ. Everything we own comes stamped with a cross, bought with the most precious blood of all. So we have no right to vow or promise anything based on our word as if we owned it.

Our words, like our lives, will be simple, honest, and true, for we are training to live happily in the family of heaven.

The Jews interpreted the third commandment to forbid using God's name profanely, but they felt free to use and take other oaths. From the words of Moses, they knew they could not give false testimony, but they had ways to make sure that what they said was technically correct, even if they knew that it was not exactly truthful. They had no problem lying under oath or misleading others as long as their words were covered by some technical definition of the law.

Jesus condemned their oath-taking, stating clearly that it was breaking God's law. But Jesus did not forbid the use of a judicial oath, which solemnly calls upon God to witness that what is said is the truth and nothing but the truth. Jesus Himself testified under a judicial oath at His trial before the Jewish court. If He condemned such oath-taking, He would have spoken against it at that time.

Many people have no problem lying to other people, but they feel much more reluctant to lie to God. Under oath, they feel as if their words are being judged by the One who reads hearts and knows the exact truth. Fear of His judgment encourages them to tell the truth.

But Christians can testify under oath with no fears. Living their lives each day in the constant presence of God, they have no problem with God being their witness that what is said is the whole truth and nothing but the truth.

Jesus saw that there was no need for oath-taking. He taught that all that was needed was speaking the exact truth at all times. "Say only yes if you mean yes, and no if you mean no. If you say more than yes or no, it is from the Evil One" (Matthew 5:37). These words should eliminate the use of meaningless phrases or near-profane expressions. There is no place for false compliments, flattering lies, gross exaggerations, scams, or deceptive trade practices. Jesus' words teach that no one can be called honest who appears to be something he is not or whose words don't tell what is really going on.

If we followed these words of Jesus, we would stop all of our unkind criticisms of others. How can we comment on another's feelings or motives and be certain that we are speaking the exact truth? Too often, pride, momentary anger, and personal resentment influence the impression we give others. A glance, a word, even the inflection of our voice, can be used to communicate a lie. Even the facts of a situation can be stated in a way that gives a

word, even the inflection of our voice, can be used to communicate a lie. Even the facts of a situation can be stated in a way that gives a false impression. And whatever is not truth is inspired by Satan.

Everything that Christians do should be as transparent as the sunlight. Truth is of God. Deception, whatever form it takes, is of Satan. Still, it is not always simple or easy to speak the exact truth.

He left heaven to bring the bread of life to His enemies, to those who would hate Him.

We cannot speak the truth unless we know the truth, but so often preconceived opinions, personal bias, a lack of information, or errors in judgment prevent us from actually understanding the situation accurately. We cannot speak the truth unless our minds are continually guided by the One who is truth.

Through the words of Paul, Jesus says, "When you talk, do not say harmful things, but say what people need—words that will help others become stronger. Then what you say will do good to those who listen to you" (Ephesians 4:29). Jesus makes it clear that pointless and unnecessary words, joking, and inappropriate conversations are to be avoided. Our words should not only be truthful, but pure and uplifting.

Those who are learning to follow Jesus will have no reason to dabble in things that are best done in secret or in darkness. Our words, like our lives, will be simple, honest, and true, for we are training to live happily in the family of heaven.

RESPONDING WITH KINDNESS

"But I tell you, don't stand up against an evil person. If someone slaps you on the right cheek, turn to him the other cheek also"
(Matthew 5:39).

The Jewish people were constantly irritated by their contact with the Roman soldiers. Rome had soldiers stationed around Judea and Galilee, and their presence reminded the people that they were a conquered nation. When they heard the loud trumpet blasts and saw the troops assemble around the banner of Rome, their souls boiled with bitterness. Frequent conflicts between the people and the soldiers inflamed the general hatred. Often, a Roman official with a soldier guard, hurrying from one point to another, would seize Jewish peasants working in the fields and force them to carry burdens up a mountainside or give some other service Roman law and custom permitted this, and any resistance by the peasants led to cruel punishment.

The people's desire to throw off Roman oppression deepened every day. The spirit of revolt was especially strong among the bold, hardworking people of Galilee. Capernaum, a border town, housed a Roman garrison. While Jesus spoke that day on the hillside, the listening people could see a company of soldiers in the distance, and this brought bitter thoughts to their minds. They looked eagerly at Jesus, hoping He was the Messiah who would drive out the hated Romans.

Jesus looked into their faces with sadness. He saw that the desire for revenge had stamped its evil mark on them. He knew how much they longed for the power to crush the Roman occupiers. Sadly, He said, "Don't stand up against an evil person. If someone slaps you on the right cheek, turn to him the other cheek also" (Matthew 5:39).

These words simply repeated the teaching of the Old Testament. It is true that one of the laws given by Moses said, " 'Eye for eye, tooth for tooth' " (Leviticus 24:20), but that was for a court of law. No one was justified in taking revenge into their own hands, because God had also said, "Don't say, 'I'll pay you back for the wrong you did.' " "Don't say, 'I'll get even.' " "If your enemy is hungry, feed him. If he is thirsty, give him a drink" (Proverbs 20:22; 24:29; 25:21).

Jesus gave His listeners a new name for the Ruler of the universe: "Our Father."

Jesus' life on this earth was a demonstration of this principle. He left heaven to bring the bread of life to His enemies, to those who would hate Him. People lied about Him and harassed Him from the cradle to the grave, but He responded only with forgiving love. The prophet Isaiah expressed it this way: "He was beaten down and punished, but he didn't say a word. He was like a lamb being led to be killed. He was quiet, as a sheep is quiet while its wool is being cut; he never opened his mouth" (Isaiah 53:7). Even on the cross, Jesus prayed for His murderers and gave a message of hope to a dying thief, a story that has been repeated over and over through the ages.

The Father's presence surrounded Jesus at all times, and nothing happened to Him except those things which were permitted by an infinite love in order to bless the world. This was Jesus' source of comfort, and it can be so for us as well. When we are filled with the spirit of Christ, we live in Him. A blow aimed at us falls instead on the Savior, who surrounds us with His presence.

Whatever happens to us comes from Jesus. We don't need to resist evil, because Jesus is our defense. Nothing can touch us without our Lord's permission, and "in everything God works for the good of those who love him" (Romans 8:28).

Every good thing we have, each ray of sunshine and shower of rain, every morsel of food, every moment of life is a gift of God's love.

"If someone wants to sue you in court and take your shirt, let him have your coat also. If someone forces you to go with him one mile, go with him two miles" (Matthew 5:40, 41). Jesus taught His disciples that instead of resisting the demands of those in authority, they should do even more than was asked of them. As far as possible, they should fulfill every request, even if it went beyond what the law required. The Law of Moses expressed great care for the poor. When a poor man had to give his cloak as security for a debt, the creditor was not permitted to go into his house and take it. He had to wait outside for the cloak to be brought to him. And whatever the situation was, the cloak must always be returned at nightfall (see Deuteronomy 24:10–13).

In Jesus' day, these merciful requirements were largely ignored, but Jesus taught His disciples to submit to the ruling of the court, even if it demanded more than the Law of Moses authorized. Even if the court demanded a part of their clothing, they should give it. They should give their creditor whatever the court authorized him to seize, and be willing to give more if necessary.

Jesus added, "If a person asks you for something, give it to him. Don't refuse to give to someone who wants to borrow from you" (Matthew 5:42). Moses had taught the same lesson: "If there are poor among you . . . do not be selfish or greedy toward them. But give freely to them, and freely lend them whatever they need" (Deuteronomy 15:7, 8). In these words, God isn't teaching us to give indiscriminately to everyone who asks for charity. The text says, "Freely lend what they need." But this should be a gift rather than a loan, since we are to "lend to them without hoping to get anything back" (Luke 6:35).

A GOD TO LOVE, NOT FEAR

"Love your enemies" (Matthew 5:44).

It was hard for the vengeful Jews to understand Jesus' teaching: "Do not stand up against an evil person" (Matthew 5:39). But now Jesus made an even stronger and more difficult statement:

God is love. Like rays of light from the sun, love and light and joy flow out from Him to all His creatures.

"You have heard that it was said, 'Love your neighbor and hate your enemies.' But I say to you, love your enemies. Pray for those who hurt you. If you do this, you will be true children of your Father in heaven" (Matthew 5:43–45).

This was the true spirit of the law that the rabbis had twisted and misinterpreted into rigid, merciless rules. They considered themselves better than other people, specially favored by God because they were Israelites. Jesus pointed them to the spirit of forgiving love that—if they followed it—would show that they were motivated, not by the idea that they were better than others, but by an even higher motivation.

Jesus gave His listeners a new name for the Ruler of the universe: "Our Father." He wanted them to understand what tender love God had for them and how He longed for them. He taught that God cares for every person, that "the LORD has mercy on those who respect him, as a father has mercy on his children" (Psalm 103:13).

This concept of God as a loving Father is unique among the religions of the world. Other religions teach that the Supreme Being should be feared rather than loved. They worship a cruel deity that needs to be appeased by sacrifices rather than a Father who showers His children with love. Since the Jews had become so blind to this precious teaching of their prophets, Jesus' revelation of God's fatherly love was a fresh new gift to the world.

The Jews taught that God loved those who served Him—that is, those who lived by the strict rules of the rabbis—but that He had only anger and curses for the rest of the world's inhabitants. "That's not true," Jesus said. "The whole world, both the evil and the good, basks in the sunshine of God's love." The Jews should have learned this truth from nature itself, for God "causes the sun to rise on good people and on evil people, and he sends rain to those who do right and to those who do wrong" (Matthew 5:45).

The earth doesn't spin and revolve around the sun year after year on its own. The hand of God guides the planets themselves and keeps them in their orbits through space. His power brings summer and winter, seedtime and harvest, day and night in their unending sequence. His word causes plants to flourish, leaves to appear, and flowers to bloom. Every good thing we have, each ray of sunshine and shower of rain, every morsel of food, every moment of life is a gift of God's love.

While we were still unkind and hateful, our heavenly Father

had mercy on us. "But when the kindness and love of God our Savior was shown, he saved us because of his mercy" (Titus 3:4, 5). If we accept His love, it will make us like Him—kind and gentle, not just to those we like, but even to the most flawed and aggravating people around us.

The children of God are those who are becoming like Him. Nationality, race, religious orientation, or church membership—none of these proves that we are members of God's family. Only love can prove that, a love that embraces all of humanity. Anyone whose heart is not completely closed to God's Spirit will respond to kindness. While a person may respond to hate with hate, he will also respond to love with love. But it is only God's Spirit that will cause a person to respond to hate with love. To be kind to the unthankful and to the evil, to do good, hoping for nothing in return—this is the insignia of heaven. This is how the children of God show their true standing in society.

PERFECT LOVE

"So you must be perfect, just as your Father in heaven is perfect"
(Matthew 5:48).

Here, the word *so* implies that the following statement refers to what has been said before. Jesus had been describing God's endless mercy and love. Then He said, "So you must be perfect." Because your heavenly Father is kind to those who are unappreciative and to those who are evil, because He has reached down and lifted you up, Jesus says that you can develop a character like His, standing without fault before others—including angels.

Today, the requirements for eternal life are just the same as they were in Eden—perfect righteousness, harmony with God, and obedience to the principles of His law. The values shown in the Old Testament are the same as those we find in the New Testament. And by God's grace we can live these values. Beneath every law, beneath every command and rule that God gives, lies a powerful promise: God has made a way by which we can become like Him. And He will make this happen for everyone who doesn't interject his or her own will and wishes in the place of God's will.

God loves us with an astounding love. As our love for Him grows, we will begin to appreciate the length and width and height and depth of this love that can never be measured. As the lovely appeal of Christ begins to be revealed, as we begin to understand the kind of love that He offers us even while we are still sinners, our stubborn hearts are melted. We can now be transformed into children of heaven. God never forces anyone—love is His tool to push sin from the human heart. With love, He changes pride into humility and turns hatred and skepticism into love and faith.

The Jews had exhausted themselves struggling to reach perfection by their own efforts—and they had failed. Christ had already told them that their kind of righteousness could never enter the kingdom of heaven. Now He points out the kind of character—the kind of righteousness—that everyone who enters heaven will possess. All through this sermon by the lake, Jesus described the outcome of this kind of character. Now, in one sentence, He points out its Source and its nature: be perfect as God is perfect. The law is just a printout of God's character. Look, your heavenly Father is a perfect example of the principles which are the foundation of His government.

God is love. Like rays of light from the sun, love and light and joy flow out from Him to all His creatures. It is His nature to give. His whole life is about unselfish love. He tells us to be perfect as He is—in the same way. We are to be centers of light and blessing to our little circle, just as God is to the universe. We have no light of our own, but the light of His love shines on us, and we can reflect it. We may be perfect in our circle just as God is perfect in His.

If we are God's children, we have His nature, so we can't help but be like Him. As a child lives because of his parents, God's children, through the rebirth of the Spirit, live because of Him. All of God—the Father, Son, and Holy Spirit—exists within Jesus, and Jesus lived in human skin. (See Colossians 2:9; 2 Corinthians 4:11.) The life of God within us will create the same character and the same behavior as it did in Jesus. In this way, we will live in harmony with every aspect of God's law. Through love, we can "be the kind of people the law correctly wants us to be. Now we do not live following our sinful selves, but we live following the Spirit" (Romans 8:4).

CHAPTER 4

THE REAL REASON TO HELP OTHERS

"Be careful! When you do good things, don't do them in front of people to be seen by them" (Matthew 6:1).

Jesus' words that day on the hillside expressed what His actions had been saying all His life, but no one had understood. They couldn't grasp how someone with His great power didn't use it to force the changes they wanted to see in their country. Their spirit and motives and methods were the opposite of His. They claimed to be very protective about honoring the law, but what they really wanted was fame and power for themselves. Jesus now made it clear to them that anyone who loves himself most is breaking the law.

But these attitudes are not unique to the Jews of Jesus' day. The spirit of the Pharisees is the spirit of human nature in all ages. As Jesus showed the differences between His own spirit and methods and those of

> *The spirit of the Pharisees is the spirit of human nature in all ages.*

the rabbis, His teaching speaks to all people, even to us today.

The Pharisees worked to be considered "holy" because in their culture, such a lifestyle was rewarded with honor and wealth—their just reward for righteousness. At the same time, they paraded their acts of charity in front of the people in order to get attention and to be thought of as righteous.

Jesus pointed out their desire to be noticed and declared that God is not impressed with such things. They might receive praise and respect from the people, but that is all they would ever get. "When you give to the poor," Jesus said, "don't let anyone know what you are doing. Your giving should be done in secret. Your Father can see what is done in secret, and he will reward you" (Matthew 6:3, 4).

We must give, not to show our generosity, but because we see the needs of others and are moved to help them.

Jesus wasn't teaching that acts of kindness should always be kept secret. The apostle Paul shared the story of the generous giving of the Macedonian Christians, but he also told how their belief in Christ had changed them. This story inspired many other Christians to give as well. Paul also wrote to the church at Corinth and said, "Your desire to give has made most of them ready to give also" (2 Corinthians 9:2).

The meaning of Jesus' words is clear: acts of kindness should not be done to impress others. Those who live for the praise and attention of others are only pretending to be Christians.

Jesus' followers bring glory to Him with their acts of kindness and generosity. Every such act is done by the influence of the Holy Spirit, and the Spirit brings glory to God, not to human beings. When the light of Christ is shining in our souls, our lips will praise and thank God. It won't be our prayers, our efforts, our generosity, or our selflessness that we'll be thinking about or discussing. Jesus will be at the center of our thoughts.

The small acts of love and self-sacrifice that flow out from a life as quietly as the fragrance from a flower are the source of much of the blessings and happiness of life.

We must give, not to show our generosity, but because we see the needs of others and are moved to help them. This kind of genuine response to those in need is what Heaven values. The person who loves others sincerely, who follows Jesus wholeheartedly, is more precious to God than pure gold.

We should think only of serving others, not of any reward, but it's true that kindness will always be rewarded. "Your Father can see what is done in secret, and he will reward you" (Matthew 6:4). A relationship with God is the greatest reward, and the more we become like Him, the more we will enjoy it. As we give ourselves in service to humanity, God gives Himself to us.

The hills and plains that provide a channel for a mountain stream to reach the sea are greatly rewarded for their gift. The singing stream leaves behind greener grass, large strong trees, and more beautiful flowers. Everywhere else the ground may lie bare and brown, but a line of rich green marks the stream's path. The plains and hills that share their space to allow the water through are blessed with freshness and beauty. In the same way, anyone who opens his or her own heart and life to be a stream of

God's blessings to the world will be richly blessed for it.

The Bible promises this blessing to those who help the poor: "Share your food with the hungry and bring poor, homeless people into your own homes. When you see someone who has no clothes, give him yours, and don't refuse to help your own relatives. Then your light will shine like the dawn, and your wounds will quickly heal. . . . The LORD will always lead you. . . . You will be like a garden that has much water, like a spring that never runs dry" (Isaiah 58:7–11).

Helping others creates a double blessing. Those who give to the needy bless others, and at the same time, are blessed even more themselves. The grace of Christ in the soul will develop unselfish character traits, traits that will purify, strengthen, and enrich the life. Secret acts of kindness will bind hearts together and will draw us closer to the heart of God, the Source of every generous thought and act. The small acts of love and self-sacrifice that flow out from a life as quietly as the fragrance from a flower are the source of much of the blessings and happiness of life. In heaven, we will find that putting the needs and happiness of others first—even if it is ridiculed here—is the true sign of a close relationship with God.

Even when kind acts are done in secret, the results in the lives of those who do them cannot be hidden. The more closely we follow Jesus and live as He did, the closer our hearts will be to God. Then by the power of the Spirit, our hearts will change and come into harmony with His. God blesses those who use the gifts He has given them. He takes great joy in blessing those who are leaning on the grace and strength of Jesus to become like Him. Those who work here on earth to develop their character by acts of kindness will "reap what they have sown" in heaven. This work, begun on earth, will continue as we develop a better, more holy life throughout eternity.

PRAY TO GOD, NOT OTHERS

"When you pray, don't be like the hypocrites" (Matthew 6:5).

The Pharisees had set hours for prayer, and if they happened to be in public at that time, they would pause wherever they were—in the street, in the market, in a crowd of people—and loudly repeat their formal, memorized prayers. Jesus strongly condemned this kind of worship, done only for show. But He wasn't speaking against public prayer. After all, Jesus prayed with His disciples and in the presence of great crowds of people. But He taught that private prayer is not a public matter. We should pray privately in our devotions, speaking only for God to hear.

In Jesus' name, we can approach God the way a small child approaches a beloved father.

No one else needs to hear our requests.

"When you pray, you should go into your room and close the door" (Matthew 6:6). We should have a place for private prayer. Jesus had special spots where He spoke with God, and so should we. We need to be able to retreat to a simple, quiet spot where we can be alone with God. "Pray to your Father who cannot be seen" (Matthew 6:6). In Jesus' name, we can approach God the way a small child approaches a beloved father. We don't need anyone to act as a go-between for us. Through Jesus, we can open our hearts to

God, certain that He knows us and loves us.

In our private place of prayer, where no one but God can see or hear us, we can pour out our most secret desires and needs to the Father of unending love. In those quiet moments, a Voice that never fails to answer the cry of human need will speak to our hearts.

"The Lord is full of mercy and is kind" (James 5:11). He waits with untiring love to hear the confessions of the rebellious and to accept their repentance. Like a mother watches for a smile of recognition from her beloved child, God watches for some indication of gratitude from us. He wants us to understand how much He loves us. He invites us to take our troubles to Him for sympathy, our sorrows to Him for comfort, our wounds to Him for healing, our weaknesses to Him for strength, and our emptiness to Him to be filled. No one has ever been disappointed by coming to Him. "Those who look to him are radiant; their faces are never covered with shame" (Psalm 34:5, NIV).

A prayer of faith is when we express our needs and desires to God in the same way we would ask a friend for a favor.

Those who seek God in secret, telling the Lord their needs and asking for His help, will always be heard. "Your Father can see what is done in secret, and he will reward you" (Matthew 6:6). When we make Jesus our constant Companion, we will feel the power of the unseen world all around us. By looking at Jesus, we will become like Him. Our characters will be softened, polished, and strengthened for the kingdom in heaven. Our prayers will become more focused and more intuitive. We are being educated by God, and this will show in our hard work and enthusiasm for the cause of Christ.

When we turn to God for help, support, and power in our sincere daily prayer, we will have a clear understanding of truth and duty, clear motives to act, and a constant desire to do good. Because we are connected to God, others, with whom we come in contact, will feel the peacefulness and joy that rule our hearts. The strength we will gain through prayer, together with our kind and gentle habits, will prepare us for each day's duties and give us peace no matter what happens.

As we come close to God, He will give us even the words we need to praise Him. He will teach us a verse from the songs of angels, who sing their gratitude to our heavenly Father. The light and love of the Savior who lives in our hearts will be shown in every action of our lives. Other worries and troubles cannot reach us as long as we are living by faith in the Son of God.

PRAYER DOES NOT PAY FOR SIN

"And when you pray, don't be like those people who don't know God"
(Matthew 6:7).

People who don't know God often see prayer itself as a way to pay for their sins. So the longer they pray the more credit they earn. If they could become holy by praying, they would have a reason to be proud of themselves. This kind of praying is a result of the principle that a person can earn his or her own salvation, which is the foundation of all false religions. The Pharisees had adopted this kind of praying, and it is not uncommon today even among those who claim to be Christians. Repeating memorized phrases when the heart feels no need of God is no different than the repetitive phrases of those who don't know God at all.

Prayer does not pay for sin. It has no value in and of itself. All the flowery words in our vocabulary are not as valuable to God as one holy desire. The most expressive prayers are just pointless words if they don't express the true feelings of

If Christians go around with a mournful attitude and give the impression that God has disappointed them, they misrepresent Him and give others reasons to doubt.

our hearts. A prayer of faith is when we express our needs and desires to God in the same way we would ask a friend for a favor. God isn't interested in our fancy words or flattery, but His heart of mercy hears the unspoken cry of any brokenhearted and repentant soul in pain.

UNDERSTANDING THE PRICE OF SIN

"When you give up eating, don't put on a sad face like the hypocrites"
(Matthew 6:16).

The fasting that Jesus recommends here is more than a ritual. It's more than just refusing to eat, wearing uncomfortable clothes, or sprinkling ashes on the head, as was the custom in Jesus' day. Real fasting shows sorrow for sin and is never done for public display or attention. When God calls us to fast, He is not trying to punish us but to help us understand the terrible nature of sin. His command to Israel was, "Tearing your clothes is not enough to show you are sad; let your heart be broken" (Joel 2:13).

It accomplishes nothing when we punish ourselves or think that we can earn a place in heaven by our own efforts. When He was asked, " 'What are the things God wants us to do?' Jesus answered, 'The work God wants you to do is this: Believe the One he sent' " (John 6:28, 29). True repentance means focusing on Christ instead of ourselves. When we accept Christ and, by faith, allow Him to live His life in us, good works will follow.

Jesus said, "But when you fast, put oil on your head and wash your face, so that it will not be obvious to men that you are fasting, but only to your Father, who is unseen; and your Father, who sees what is done in secret, will reward you" (Matthew 6:17, 18, NIV). Whatever is done for God's glory should be done with joy, not with sadness and despair. The religion of Jesus isn't gloomy or miserable. If Christians go around with a mournful attitude and give the impression that God has disappointed them, they mis-

Others may never know the work going on secretly between our souls and God, but the results, the changes in our lives, will be seen by all.

represent Him and give others reasons to doubt. Even if they claim God as their Father, their gloom and sadness makes them look to the world like spiritual orphans.

Jesus wants the world to see the joy we find in following Him.

We can share our troubles and disappointments with the Savior and not those around us. We can leave our burdens with Jesus and go our way rejoicing in His love. Others may never know the work going on secretly between our souls and God, but the results, the changes in our lives, will be seen by all. "Your Father sees what is done in secret, and he will reward you" (Matthew 6:18).

> *The followers of Jesus are called His jewels, His treasure.*

TREASURES IN HEAVEN

"Don't store treasures for yourselves here on earth" (Matthew 6:19).

Treasures stored on earth do not last. Our precious possessions here can be stolen by thieves, eaten away by rust or moths, or destroyed by fire or storms. "Your heart will be where your treasure is," Jesus said (Matthew 6:21). Worrying over our possessions here can turn our minds away from heavenly things.

> *True holiness begins when we are no longer satisfied with . . . half-hearted devotion to God.*

The love of money was the driving force of the Jewish age. Possessions and power took the place of God and religion in the people's hearts. And that still happens today. Greed for wealth can captivate a person, corrupting him until he is selfish, cold, and mean. This is serving Satan and brings only worry, confusion, and stress as the treasure that is pursued quickly disappears.

Jesus said, "Store your treasures in heaven where they cannot be destroyed by moths or rust and where thieves cannot break in and steal them. Your heart will be where your treasure is" (Matthew 6:20, 21). The treasure you store in heaven is really the only thing you possess, but it cannot be stolen or destroyed. Fire, flood, thief, moth, or rust cannot touch it, because God is keeping it safe.

Jesus considers the most precious treasure to be His people. The followers of Jesus are called His jewels, His treasure. He says, "They will shine in his land like jewels in a crown" (Zechariah 9:16). He sees His people, in their purity and perfection, as His reward for all His suffering, for all His love. They reflect His glory.

God never gives up on anyone as long as there is any hope of saving that person.

And we can join His work and share the riches His death purchased. The apostle Paul wrote to the believers at Thessalonica: "You are our hope, our joy, and the crown we will take pride in when our Lord Jesus Christ comes. Truly you are our glory and our joy" (1 Thessalonians 2:19, 20). This is the treasure Jesus invites us to work for. Our character is what we take from this life. Everything that we do or say that leads another person to reach toward heaven, every effort we put into forming a character like Jesus' character, is treasure we are storing in heaven.

Our hearts will be with our treasure, wherever it is. Every time we work to help another person, we help ourselves. When we give money or time to spread the gospel, when we pray for others, we are showing our interest in God's work and those who may be reached by it. We find ourselves more devoted to spending time with God so that we can find ways to help others more effectively.

At the end of time, when all of earth's wealth has been destroyed, the person who has stored his treasure in heaven will see what his life has accomplished. Someday, we will see those who have been saved because of our efforts. We will know that each of them has reached out to others, and those to still others, and finally we will see the entire crowd of people who are in heaven praising God because of what we did. What a joy it will be to meet them and join with them in praising the Savior! How precious heaven will be to us if we faithfully work to reach others!

> *All created things resonate with the pulse of life from the great heart of God.*

"Since you were raised from the dead with Christ, aim at what is in heaven, where Christ is sitting at the right hand of God" (Colossians 3:1).

BLINDED BY SELFISHNESS

"If your eyes are good, your whole body will be full of light" (Matthew 6:22).

We need focused, wholehearted devotion to God. If it is our intention to understand God's truth and follow it, then we will be given divine light to help our search. True holiness begins when we are no longer satisfied with a life of compromise with sin and half-hearted devotion to God. Then our hearts will say along with the apostle Paul, "There is one thing I always do. Forgetting the past and straining toward what is ahead, I keep trying to reach the goal and get the prize for which God called me through Christ to the life above" (Philippians 3:13, 14).

But when our eyes are blinded by selfishness, only darkness remains. "But if your eyes are evil, your whole body will be full of darkness" (Matthew 6:23). This was the darkness that left the Jews refusing to believe, making it impossible for them to understand who Jesus was and why He came to earth.

We give in to temptation when our minds begin to waver and we forget to trust in God. If we don't choose to give ourselves completely to God, then we are in darkness. When we hold back in any area, we leave open a door for Satan to enter and entice us with temptation. He knows that if he can block our vision—our faith in God—then nothing will keep us from following him into sin.

The more often we follow our sinful desires, the more blind our souls become. Every time we indulge in sin, we are pulled further from God. As we follow this path of Satan's, we walk further into the shadow of evil, and every step leads into deeper darkness, into greater blindness.

It's the same in the spiritual world as it is in the natural world. A person who lives in darkness will eventually lose the ability to see. He or she will be covered by a darkness deeper than midnight until even the brightest ray of sunlight can do nothing to change it. He or she "lives in darkness, and does not know where to go, because the darkness has made that person blind" (1 John 2:11). If we constantly choose evil, if we ignore the call of God's love, we will lose our love for things that are good, our interest in God, and our ability to see the light from heaven. God's call of love still goes out to us; the Light is still shining as brightly as it did the day we first felt His love. But God's voice falls on deaf ears, and His light shines on blind eyes.

God never gives up on anyone as long as there is any hope of saving that person. We turn away from God; God doesn't turn away from us. Our heavenly Father pursues us with warnings of danger and promises of mercy as long as we will listen. But we make that decision. If we resist God's Spirit today, we will find it easier to resist it tomorrow. And so our resistance increases until we don't respond to the Holy Spirit at all. Then, whatever light we had in our heart becomes darkness. The truths we do know become so twisted that they make us blinder than ever.

NO MIDDLE GROUND

"No one can serve two masters" (Matthew 6:24).

Jesus doesn't say that we won't serve two masters. He doesn't say we shouldn't serve two masters. He says that we *can't* serve two masters. Our human selfishness has nothing in common with the selfless love of God. At the very spot where a nonbeliever readily steps forward to act on his selfish tendencies, a Christian's conscience will warn him to wait, to say No, to stop. On one side is the selfless follower of Jesus; on the other side is the selfish lover of pleasure, caving in to fashion and wasting time in all types of meaningless actions. True Christians cannot cross that line.

No one can be neutral; no one can stand in the middle, neither loving God nor serving Satan. Jesus will live in the hearts of His followers, working through them. With their will tied to His will, they will act with His Spirit. Jesus now lives in them. A Christian who isn't totally committed to God is under the control of another power, listening to another voice. Half-hearted commitment leaves the believer in the enemy's camp. And when those who claim to be believers end up helping Satan, they become enemies of Jesus. They open a path for Satan to tempt other Christians and steal their hearts as well.

It's not the wicked life of the wild sinner or the corrupt outcast that causes the most evil in this world. It's the person who appears to be righteous and honorable, but who is actually holding on to one sin. Their example is a very powerful excuse to give in for those who are struggling on the very edge of temptation. A person who knows truth, who understands what it means to be honorable and moral, but who still chooses to go against one of God's laws, has turned God's gifts—genius, talent, sympathy, even kindness—into a trap to lead others to ruin their lives and their chance of heaven.

"Do not love the world or the things in the world. If you love the world, the love of the Father is not in you. These are the ways of the world: wanting to please our sinful selves, wanting the sinful things we see, and being too proud of what we have. None of these come from the Father, but all of them come from the world" (1 John 2:15, 16).

THE BIRDS AND THE FLOWERS

"So I tell you, don't worry" (Matthew 6:25).

God, who has given us life, knows that we need food to sustain it. He created our bodies, so He knows we need clothing. Can't we trust the One who made us to make sure we have what we need?

In the warm sunshine that day on the hillside, Jesus pointed out the birds singing their joyous songs without a thought or worry about their next meal. "Your heavenly Father feeds them," He said. "And you know that you are worth much more than the birds" (Matthew 6:26).

The hillside and fields around them were bright with flowers still sparkling with the morning dew. "Look at how the lilies in the field grow" (Matthew 6:28), Jesus said to the crowd. The graceful forms and delicate colors of plants and flowers can be modeled and copied by humans, but even the most perfect

Why has He given us singing birds and gentle blossoms? Because His heart is overflowing with a Father's love, and He longs to make our days brighter and more joyful.

of re-creations lacks the spark of life. Every blossom owes its existence to the same Power that flung out the stars and planets. All created things resonate with the pulse of life from the great heart of God. The flowers of the fields are clothed more beautifully than any king or queen wearing expensive garments. "God clothes the grass in the field, which is alive today but tomorrow is thrown into the fire. So you can be even more sure that God will clothe you. Don't have so little faith!" (Matthew 6:30).

The One who painted the flowers and gave the sparrow its song says, "Look at the birds and the lilies." In the beauty of nature we can learn more about the wisdom of God than learned scholars can know. On the petals of the lily, God has a message for us. It is written in a language that our hearts can read only as we let go of doubt and selfishness. Why has He given us singing birds and gentle blossoms? Because His heart is overflowing with a Father's love, and He longs to make our days brighter and more joyful. We don't need the beauty of the flowers or birds in order to exist, but God wasn't content to have us just survive. He filled the earth and air and sky with objects and creatures of amazing beauty just to communicate His love for us. The beauty of all created things is only a reflected glimpse of His glory. And seeing that He has invested such miraculous skill in nature just for our happiness, how can we doubt that He will give us everything we need?

Every flower that opens its petals to the sunshine obeys the same great laws that guide the stars. God uses the flowers to call our attention to the beauty of a character like the character of Jesus. The One who gave such beauty to the blossoms wants even more for our souls to be painted with a character like His.

Teach them that He wants their lives to be beautiful like the flowers.

Jesus said to look at how the lilies grow, how even though they spring up from the cold, dark ground or from the mud at a river's edge, they produce such loveliness and fragrance. Who could imagine that such beauty was contained in a rough, brown bulb? In the same way, few can imagine that a rough, unkind person can unfold into a generous, joyous individual when touched by God's love. The life and love of God will spring out of every person who gives himself to Him.

God's law is the law of love. He surrounds us with beauty to teach us that we are not placed on earth just to serve ourselves and our own interests. We are here to make life bright and joyful and beautiful for everyone around us. Like flowers, we can cheer the lives of others with the love of Christ.

Parents, let your children learn from the flowers. Take them with you into a garden or field or under a leafy tree, and teach them to read the message of God's love in nature. Link their thoughts of God with the birds and flowers and trees. Show them that every fascinating and beautiful thing in nature is an expression of God's love for them. Let them see the joy you find in your belief in God. Define your religion with kindness.

God's arms are wrapped around those that turn to Him for help, no matter how weak they may be.

Teach them that God's great love makes it possible for people—including them—to become more like Jesus every day. Teach them that He wants their lives to be beautiful like the flowers. As they gather the blossoms, teach them that the Creator is even lovelier than His creations. This way, the "vines" of their hearts will become wrapped around His. He will be a daily Companion and Friend to them, and they will grow more and more like Him.

WHAT REALLY MATTERS

"The thing you should want most is God's kingdom" (Matthew 6:33).

The people who were listening that day were still anxiously watching for Jesus to announce His kingdom on earth. While Jesus taught them about the treasures of heaven, many were thinking, *How will He make our nation more powerful?* Jesus wanted to help them understand that by making the concerns of this world their highest priority they were living as if there were no God—just like the heathen nations around them were doing.

"The people who don't know God keep trying to get these things, and your Father in heaven knows you need them. The thing you should want most is God's kingdom and doing what God wants. Then all these other things you need will be given to you" (Matthew 6:32, 33). "I have come to show you the kingdom of love and righteousness and peace," Jesus said. "Open your hearts and accept this kingdom and focus on it instead of this world. It is a spiritual kingdom, but don't worry about your earthly needs. If you serve God, He has all the power of heaven and earth to meet your needs."

Jesus doesn't excuse us from the need to work hard. He teaches us to make Him the focus of everything we do. We shouldn't pursue any work, any interests, any recreation or amusement that would hold back the development of His righteousness in our lives. Whatever we do, we should do it energetically, like we're doing it for God Himself.

God knows the end from the beginning. We cannot see what will happen tomorrow, but He can.

In His life on earth, Jesus lived with dignity, always showing others what God was like, always following His Father's plan precisely. And He assures us that if we live this way, He will give us everything we need. Whether we are wealthy or poor, healthy or sick, wise or simpleminded, His grace will provide all we need.

God's arms are wrapped around those that turn to Him for help, no matter how weak they may be. The things we consider precious—diamonds, silver, gold—will someday dissolve, but the person who lives for God will live forever. "The world and everything that people want in it are passing away, but the person who does what God wants lives forever" (1 John 2:17). The city of God will be open to those who learned on earth that they could trust God for guidance and wisdom and comfort and hope, even in times of great sadness and pain. The songs of angels will welcome them, and the tree of life will share its fruit. " 'The mountains may disappear, and the hills may come to an end, but my love will never disappear; my promise of peace will not come to an end,' says the LORD who shows mercy to you" (Isaiah 54:10).

TOMORROW HAS ITS OWN WORRIES

"So don't worry about tomorrow, because tomorrow will have its own worries. Each day has enough trouble of its own" (Matthew 6:34).

If we give ourselves to God and commit ourselves to do His work, then we don't need to worry about tomorrow. God knows the end from the beginning. We cannot see what will happen tomorrow, but He can.

When we take control of our own lives and depend on our own wisdom for success, we are doing something God hasn't asked us to do and are trying to do it without His help. We have taken to ourselves the responsibility that should be God's. We have put ourselves in His place. This will, indeed, create anxiety about possible danger and failure because we are on a sure path to disaster.

But when we really believe that God loves us and wants us to succeed, we'll stop worrying over the future. We'll trust God the way a child trusts a loving parent. Then our troubles and problems will disappear because we will want only what God wants.

Jesus didn't promise to help us carry tomorrow's burdens today. He says, "My grace is enough for you" (2 Corinthians 12:9), but, like the manna the Israelites received in the wilderness, His grace is given daily, for each day's problems. Like the Israelites on their long journey, we will discover the "bread" we need each day.

We are given only one day at a time, and for that one day, we can live for God. We can place our one day in Jesus' hands, giving Him both our plans and our worries. " 'I say this because I know what I am planning for you,' says the LORD. 'I have good plans for you, not plans to hurt you. I will give you hope and a good future' " (Jeremiah 29:11).

If we commit ourselves to the Lord each day, choosing to be free and happy as we obey and serve Him, all our worries will be stilled, all our issues settled, all our confusing problems solved.

CHAPTER 5

"OUR FATHER"

"So when you pray, you should pray like this" (Matthew 6:9).

Jesus shared what we call the Lord's Prayer twice: once with the crowd on the hillside in Galilee, and later with the disciples alone. On that occasion, the disciples had been away from Jesus for a short time, and when they returned, they found Him praying. Seemingly unaware of their presence, Jesus continued speaking out loud to His Father. Such a brightness shone on His face that He seemed to be in God's very presence, and the power in His words made it clear that He was talking with the King of heaven.

The disciples were deeply moved. They noticed how often Jesus spent long hours with His Father in prayer. His days were filled with ministry to the demanding crowds and in exposing the lies of the rabbis. This constant work often left Him so exhausted that His mother and brothers and the disciples were afraid He would die. But Jesus always found time to pray at the end of the long days, and when He returned from praying, the disciples would see peace on His face and sense that He was refreshed. It was the hours He spent with God in prayer that al-

freshed. It was the hours He spent with God in prayer that allowed Jesus to step out, morning after morning, to share the light of heaven with men and women. The disciples saw the connection between His hours of prayer and the power of His words and actions. Now, as they listened to Him in prayer, their hearts were filled with wonder and humility. When He finished praying, they couldn't help but ask, "Lord, teach us to pray" (Luke 11:1).

Jesus didn't teach them a new way to pray. He repeated what He had taught before, as if to say, "You need to understand the things I have already shared. There is meaning here that you don't yet understand."

In giving this model prayer, Jesus isn't saying that we should use only these words when we pray. Being human Himself, He shared His own way to pray, a prayer with words so simple that even a child can say and understand them, but so deep that the greatest mind cannot fully appreciate their meaning. His words teach us to come to God first with our gratitude and praise, then to express our wants and needs, to confess our shortcomings, and to claim the mercy He has promised.

> *It was the hours He spent with God in prayer that allowed Jesus to step out, morning after morning, to share the light of heaven with men and women.*

"HIS FATHER IS OUR FATHER"

"When you pray, say 'Father' " (Luke 11:2).

Jesus teaches us to call *His* Father our Father. He is not ashamed to call us brothers and sisters. He is so willing, so anxious to welcome us as members of His family that He makes our relationship clear in these first words we are to use in addressing God: "Our Father."

Here Jesus reveals a most wonderful truth: God loves us just as He loves His Son! This is what Jesus said in His last prayer for His disciples: "You loved them just as much as you loved me" (John 17:23).

This world that Satan had claimed and ruled over and dominated with cruelty was surrounded by Jesus' love and connected again to the throne of God. Angels and the inhabitants of sinless worlds sang anthems of praise when this victory was certain. They rejoiced that the path of salvation had been opened to people on earth and that the planet would be saved from the curse of sin. Shouldn't we celebrate even more?

Here Jesus reveals a most wonderful truth: God loves us just as He loves His Son!

How can we continue to be in doubt, uncertain of God's acceptance, feeling that we are orphans? Jesus became human to save the very ones who had sinned and broken the law. He became like us so that we could have eternal peace and the assurance of God's love. We have a human representative in heaven, and if we accept Him as our Savior, we will not be left alone like orphans to carry our own load of sin.

"If we are God's children, we will receive blessings from God together with Christ. But we must suffer as Christ suffered so that we will have glory as Christ has glory" (Romans 8:17).

The very first step in approaching God is to believe that He loves us. It is His love that draws us to Him. Understanding God's love for us is the antidote to selfishness. When we call God "Father," we are calling all of His children our brothers and sisters. We are all part of the great web of humanity, all members of one family. Realizing this, we include our neighbors as well as ourselves when we pray, since true prayer is never selfish, asking only for personal blessings.

The infinite God allows us to speak to Him as Father. Understand what that means. No human parents ever plead so sincerely with a disobedient child as God pleads with you. No human ever pursued the rebellious with such tender invitations to be saved. God lives in every home, hearing every word that is spoken, listening to every prayer, feeling the sorrow and disappointment of every person. He sees how fathers, mothers, brothers, sisters, friends, and neighbors are treated. His love and mercy and grace are continually flowing to meet our needs.

When we call God "Father," we are calling all of His children our brothers and sisters.

But if we call God our Father, we acknowledge that we are His children, guided by His wisdom, obedient to His will, secure in the knowledge that His love will never change. We will accept His plan for our lives. As children of God, we will see His honor, His character, His family, His work, as the center of our being. It will be our joy to recognize and honor our relationship to our

Father and to every member of His family. We will be delighted to do any task, no matter how unimportant, that will reflect His glory or increase the well-being of our brothers and sisters.

Jesus invites us to look at God as our Father in heaven (Matthew 6:9), and as the psalmist says, "Our God is in heaven. He does what he pleases" (Psalm 115:3). We can feel safe and secure when we are in our Father's care, saying, "When I am afraid, I will trust you" (Psalm 56:3).

GOD'S HOLY NAME

" 'May your name always be kept holy' " (Matthew 6:9).

We keep God's name holy when we speak of the King of the universe with reverence and respect. We should never treat the name or titles of God lightly or frivolously. When we pray, we should enter His presence with a holy sense of wonder and admiration. The angels themselves cover their faces in His presence. Even the leaders of the angels approach His throne with quiet

> *In everything we do, we display God's name.*

reverence. Shouldn't we, as mortal, sinful beings, come to our Lord and Creator reverently?

But to keep God's name holy means even more than this. Like the Jews in Jesus' day, we can show great reverence for God outwardly, but still be completely irreverent in our actions by not showing His mercy and faithfulness. "The LORD is a God who shows mercy, who is kind, who doesn't become angry quickly, who has great love and faithfulness. . . . The LORD forgives people for evil, for sin, and for turning against him" (Exodus

34:6, 7). The church, which bears the Lord's name, should reflect His love. We should be called by the same name that He is. The prophet Jeremiah, in a time of great trouble for Israel, prayed, "We are called by your name so don't leave us without help!" (Jeremiah 14:9).

God's name is kept holy by the angels of heaven and by the people of sinless worlds. When we pray, "May your name always be kept holy," we are asking that it be kept holy in this world as well. To the world and to the angels of heaven, God acknowledges us as His children. Let us do nothing to dishonor His name. God sends us into the world as His representatives. In everything we do, we display God's name. Here, Jesus asks us to display His character as well. We cannot keep God's name holy or represent Him unless our actions and character are like His. And this we can do only by accepting Jesus' grace and righteousness as our own.

A KINGDOM IN US

" 'May your kingdom come' " (Matthew 6:10).

God is our Father; He loves and cares for us as His children. He is also the great King of the universe. The concerns of His kingdom are our concerns, and we must work to build it up.

The disciples of Jesus were looking for His kingdom to begin immediately, but by giving them this prayer, Jesus taught them that this was not going happen. They were to pray for its coming as an event in the future. But at the same time, this assured them that while the kingdom might not be coming in their day, it was surely coming.

The kingdom of God's grace is being built day by day as people who have been deep in sin and rebellion choose to accept His love. But the kingdom of God's glory won't be fully revealed until Jesus returns to this world. " 'Then the holy people who belong to the Most High God will have the power to rule. They will rule over all the kingdoms under heaven with power and greatness, and their power to rule will last forever' " (Daniel 7:27). God's people will inherit the kingdom created for them from the beginning. Jesus will then assume His throne and His great power.

> *God's kingdom will not come until the good news of His love has been taken to the entire world.*

On that day, the gates of heaven will open and with millions of His angels, Jesus will ride forth as King of kings and Lord of lords. "Then the LORD will be king over the whole world. At that time there will be only one LORD, and his name will be the only name" (Zechariah 14:9). "Now God's presence is with people, and he will live with them, and they will be his people. God himself will be with them and will be their God" (Revelation 21:3).

But before that day arrives, Jesus said, "The Good News about God's kingdom will be preached in all the world, to every nation" (Matthew 24:14). God's kingdom will not come until the good news of His love has been taken to the entire world. Therefore, when we give our lives to God and lead others to accept Him, we are bringing the day of His kingdom closer. Those who are sincerely praying, "May your kingdom come," are truly dedicated to God's cause, to working for others " 'so that they may turn away from darkness to the light, away from the power of

Satan and to God. Then their sins can be forgiven, and they can have a place with those people who have been made holy by believing in me' " (Acts 26:18).

THE PRINCIPLES OF HEAVEN

" 'May . . . what you want be done, here on earth as it is in heaven' "
(Matthew 6:10).

God's will is expressed in His law. The principles of this law are the principles of heaven. Angels want nothing more than to know God's will, and to serve Him is their highest honor. But in heaven, their service is never given in a spirit of legalism. When Satan rebelled against God's law, the angels were almost shocked to realize that a law even existed. Angels work as sons of God, not as servants. They are in perfect harmony with their Creator. Obedience is not a chore to them because their love for God makes serving Him a joy. The same can be true for us, and we can also speak the words of the psalmist, "My God, I want to do what you want. Your teachings are in my heart" (Psalm 40:8).

The appeal, " 'May . . . what you want be done, here on earth as it is in heaven' " is a prayer that the reign of evil on this earth will end, that sin will be destroyed forever, and that the kingdom of righteousness will begin.

ALL WE NEED EACH DAY

" 'Give us the food we need for each day' " (Matthew 6:11).

The first half of Jesus' model prayer deals with the name and the kingdom and the will of God. After putting God's service first, we can confidently ask that our own needs be granted. When we have set selfishness aside and dedicated ourselves to following Jesus, we can know that we are members of God's family and that everything in our Father's house is ours. All of God's treasures are available to us, both in this world today and in the world to come. The ministry of angels, the gift of the Holy Spirit, and the work of God's followers—all these are for us. The world and everything in it is ours, as long as it is good for us. Even the hatred of the wicked will be a blessing by preparing us for heaven. If you belong to Christ, then "all things belong to you" (1 Corinthians 3:21).

> *God gives to us so that we can feed those who are hungry. This is how God cares for the poor.*

Like a child who is not yet allowed to control an inherited fortune, God does not yet give us our most precious possessions. Jesus keeps them for us, safely out of Satan's reach. Like a child, we will receive each day just what we need. Every day we are to pray, "Give us the food we need for each day." We don't need to worry about having enough for tomorrow. As David said, "I was young, and now I am old, but I have never seen good people left helpless or their children begging for food" (Psalm 37:25). The same God who sent ravens to feed Elijah as he hid by the brook Cherith will meet the needs of His faithful, self-sacrificing children today. Of these faithful children, the Bible says, "He will always have bread, and he will not run out of water" (Isaiah 33:16); "He did not spare his own Son but gave him for us all. So with Jesus, God will surely give us all things" (Romans 8:32).

Jesus lightened the cares and worries of His widowed mother

in her effort to care for her household in Nazareth. And this same Jesus sympathizes with every mother who struggles to care for her family. The same Jesus who felt sorry for the crowd because they were "hurting and helpless" (Matthew 9:36), still has compassion for the miserable and poor today. He reaches out to bless them and in this model prayer, He teaches us to remember the unfortunate as well.

When we pray, "Give us the food we need for each day," we are asking for others as well as ourselves. And we realize that what God gives us is not for us alone. God gives to us so that we can feed those who are hungry. This is how God cares for the poor. He says, "When you give a lunch or a dinner, don't invite only your friends, your family, your other relatives, and your rich neighbors. . . . Instead, when you give a feast, invite the poor, the crippled, the lame, and the blind. Then you will be blessed, because they have nothing and cannot pay you back. But you will be repaid when the good people rise from the dead" (Luke 14:12–14).

No matter how badly someone has hurt us, we shouldn't hold on to our offended feelings. We should forgive that person the way we would want God to forgive us.

The prayer for daily food includes more than just physical food to maintain the body. It also asks for spiritual food that will nourish the soul. Jesus counsels us, "Don't work for the food that spoils. Work for the food that stays good always and gives eternal life" (John 6:27). He says, "I am the living bread that came down from heaven. Anyone who eats this bread will live forever" (verse 51). Our Savior is the

Bread of Life. By absorbing His love, by accepting it into our souls, we eat the bread of heaven.

We learn of Jesus through His Word. The Holy Spirit was given to us to help us understand the Bible and apply its truths to our lives. If we pray each day as we read His Word, God will send His Spirit to open our minds to truths that will strengthen our souls.

By teaching us to ask every day for our physical and spiritual needs, God helps us understand that we depend on Him to supply all our needs. As we pray and study the great truths of the Bible, we will be like hungry souls that are fed. We will drink at the Fountain of life and be refreshed. This is the relationship He wants to have with us.

MORE THAN FORGIVEN

" *Forgive us for our sins, just as we have forgiven those who sinned against us' " (Matthew 6:12).*

Jesus teaches that God can forgive us only if we forgive others. It is God's love that draws us to Him, and that love cannot touch our hearts without creating a love for those around us.

After giving the Lord's Prayer, Jesus added, "Yes, if you forgive others for their sins, your Father in heaven will also forgive you for your sins. But if you don't forgive others, your Father in heaven will not forgive your sins" (Matthew 6:14, 15). If we don't forgive, we cut off the channel through which God can forgive us. Just because someone hasn't confessed or asked us for forgiveness doesn't mean that we are justified to withhold our forgiveness. Yes, that person should repent and confess, but we should offer him the same kindness, the same forgiveness, whether or not he does. No matter how badly someone has hurt us, we shouldn't hold on to our offended feelings. We should forgive that person the way we would want God to forgive us.

Forgiveness means much more than most imagine. When God promises through the prophet Isaiah that He will "freely forgive," He indicates that the promise includes more than we can comprehend: "My thoughts are not like your thoughts. Your ways are not like my ways. Just as the heavens are higher than the earth, so are my ways higher than your ways and my thoughts higher than your thoughts" (Isaiah 55:7–9). God's forgiveness is not simply a judicial pardon. He not only forgives us—He reclaims us. The impact of His saving love transforms our hearts. David had the right idea about forgiveness when he prayed, "Create in me a pure heart, God, and make my spirit right again" (Psalm 51:10).

Accepting God's love and mercy comes with only one condition: we must share that love with others.

God—through Jesus—gave Himself to pay for our sins. He suffered a cruel death on the cross and carried a burden of guilt to show us His love and draw us back to Him. And He says, "Be kind and loving to each other, and forgive each other just as God forgave you in Christ" (Ephesians 4:32). If we allow Jesus to live in us, we will be able to be a channel of the kind of heaven-born love that will give hope to the hopeless and peace to those who are stressed with sin. Accepting God's love and mercy comes with only one condition: we must share that love with others.

In order to accept and share the forgiving love of God, we must believe it and trust that it is real. Satan is working constantly to keep us doubting. He will lead us to think that our mistakes are so terrible that God will not listen to our prayers, bless us, or save us. Satan will try to make us feel that there is nothing in us but weakness, nothing of value to God, and he will tell us that there's no reason even to try—we can't fix our defects of character. When we think of praying to God, Satan will whisper, "Why bother? You know you've done evil things, sinning against God and violating your own conscience."

But we can tell Satan that "the blood of Jesus, God's Son, cleanses us from every sin" (1 John 1:7). When we feel that we've sinned and cannot pray, that's when we most need to pray. We may be ashamed and humiliated, but we must pray and believe. Along with Paul we can say, "What I say is true, and you should fully accept it: Christ Jesus came into the world to save sinners, of whom I am the worst" (1 Timothy 1:15). Forgiveness doesn't come to us as a reward for something we've done or because of our goodness. It's a gift given to us because of the perfect goodness of Christ.

We shouldn't try to escape our guilt by finding excuses for our sin. We need to accept the price God puts on sin—the price paid on Calvary. The weight of our sins would crush us, but Jesus, sinless Jesus, took our place and paid our penalty. "If we confess our sins, he will forgive our sins, because we can trust God to do what is right. He will cleanse us from all the wrongs we have done" (1 John 1:9). How wonderful to know that God both keeps His own laws and pardons everyone who believes in Jesus! "There is no God like you. You forgive those who are guilty of sin; you don't look at the sins of your people who are left alive. You will not stay angry forever, because you enjoy being kind" (Micah 7:18).

THE ANTIDOTE TO TEMPTATION
" 'And do not cause us to be tempted, but save us from the Evil One' "
(Matthew 6:13).

Temptation is an invitation to sin, and it comes from Satan and our own hearts, not from God. "Evil cannot tempt God, and God himself does not tempt anyone" (James 1:13).

Satan tries to claim that we are his followers; he tempts us in order to show our weaknesses to other humans and to the angels. In Zechariah's symbolic prophecy, Satan stands to the right of the Angel of the Lord, accusing Joshua, the high priest, who is clothed in filthy rags and resisting what the Angel wants him to do. This is a picture of Satan's plan for every human who is trying to follow Christ. He leads us to sin, and then uses that very sin as evidence that we aren't worthy of God's love. But "the LORD said to Satan, 'The LORD says no to you, Satan! The LORD who has chosen Jerusalem says no to you! This man was like a burning stick pulled from the fire.'. . . Then the angel said to Joshua, 'Look, I have taken away your sin from you, and I am giving you beautiful, fine clothes' " (Zechariah 3:2–4).

Our only defense against evil is the presence of Jesus in our hearts.

Because of His great love, God is working to develop a reflection of His Spirit in us. He allows us to face problems, persecution, and suffering, not as a curse but as the greatest blessing of our lives. Every time we resist a temptation or bravely face a problem, we gain a new understanding of life and our character grows and matures. When we resist temptation through the power of Christ, we show the world and the universe the power of God's grace.

Bitter troubles should not discourage us. But we should pray that God will keep us safe from the sinful desires of our own hearts. When we pray this prayer that Jesus gave us, we put ourselves in God's hands and ask Him to protect us, even from ourselves. We can't sincerely offer this prayer and still decide to go our own way. We must wait for His hand to lead us. We must listen to His voice, saying, "This is the right way. You should go this way" (Isaiah 30:21).

It's not safe for us to imagine what might be if we gave in to Satan's suggestions. Sin always brings dishonor and disaster, but it's often attractively disguised. If we wander off into Satan's territory, we may find ourselves unprotected from his power. As far as is possible, we must shut off every path that Satan can take to reach us.

The prayer, "Do not cause us to be tempted," is actually a promise. If we dedicate ourselves to God, we can be sure that He "will not permit you to be tempted more than you can stand. But when you are tempted, he will also give you a way to escape so that you will be able to stand it" (1 Corinthians 10:13).

Our only defense against evil is the presence of Jesus in our hearts. Temptations have power over us because of our selfishness. But selfishness looks hideous and repulsive next to the great love of God, and we will want to be rid of it. As the Holy Spirit lifts the love of Christ up to us, our hearts are changed, temptation loses its attraction, and our characters are transformed.

Jesus will never give up on anyone. We may turn away from

Him and be overwhelmed with temptation, but He will never turn away from us. After all, He gave His life for us. If we were able to perceive the spiritual realm, we would see people weighed down with grief, broken, and ready to die of discouragement. We would see angels flying swiftly to the side of those who are standing on the brink of temptation. These angels force back the agents of evil that surround them and guide them to safe ground. The battles fought between angels of heaven and Satan's demons are as real as any war on earth, and they affect the eternal destiny of all.

As Jesus said to Peter, so He says to us, "Satan has asked to test all of you as a farmer sifts his wheat. I have prayed that you will not lose your faith!" (Luke 22:31, 32). But thank God, we are not alone. God will never desert us in our battle with Satan, because He "loved the world so much that he gave his one and only Son so that whoever believes in him may not be lost, but have eternal life" (John 3:16).

Live in constant contact with Jesus. He will hold us by the hand and will never let go. Know and believe that God loves us. By doing so, we are safe. God's love is an unconquerable fortress, secure from any attacks by Satan. "The LORD is like a strong tower; those who do right can run to him for safety" (Proverbs 18:10).

THE ULTIMATE AUTHORITY, POWER, AND GLORY

"For [yours] is the kingdom, and the power, and the glory"
(Matthew 6:13, KJV).

Like the first sentence in the Lord's Prayer, the last one points to God as the ultimate Authority, Power, and Glory in the universe. At that moment, Jesus was looking forward into the years ahead for His disciples. They dreamed of days of wealth and honor in the Messiah's kingdom, but instead they would find human hatred and satanic fury. During their nation's fighting and destruction, the disciples would be in danger and would often have good reason to be afraid. They would live to see Jerusalem destroyed, the temple demolished, and the people of Israel scattered to many countries. Jesus said, "You will hear about wars and stories of wars that are coming. . . . Nations will fight against other nations; kingdoms will fight against other kingdoms. There will be times when there is no food for people to eat, and there will be earthquakes in different places" (Matthew 24:6, 7).

But these believers had no reason to fear that their hope was lost or that God had given up on the earth. There was no chance that the plans of One with such power and glory could be stopped. In this prayer for their daily needs, the followers of Jesus were reminded to look past the apparent power of established evil and see the Lord whose kingdom rules over all and who is their Father and Friend.

God never sleeps, and He will carry out His own work.

The destruction of Jerusalem was a symbol of the final destruction of the world. The prophecies partially fulfilled by the capture and destruction of Jerusalem will be completely fulfilled in the last days. We stand today on the verge of great and solemn events. A crisis is coming, worse than any the world has ever seen. But we have the same sweet assurance the disciples did, the assurance that God's kingdom has power over all others. Our Creator holds the schedule of upcoming events. He takes into account not only His church, but the people of all nations, as He brings the rule of sin in the world to a close.

In the prophet Ezekiel's vision, a hand appeared beneath the wings of angels. This was to teach God's messengers that His power is always working for them and is what brings them success. God's work does not depend on any single person and He doesn't burden His messengers with such responsibility. God never sleeps, and He will carry out His own work. He will spoil the plans of the wicked and will confuse the words of those who plot against His people. The King of the universe, the Lord of the angels, watches over His children. Our Savior rules the heavens. He is aware of every problem and trial we face. Even if nations fall and the weapons of war are striking His enemies, His followers will be safe in His hands.

"LORD, you are great and powerful. You have glory, victory, and honor. Everything in heaven and on earth belongs to you. . . . You have the power and strength to make anyone great and strong" (1 Chronicles 29:11, 12).

CHAPTER 6

TRUE CHRISTIANITY

"Don't judge other people, or you will be judged" (Matthew 7:1).

When human beings try to work for and earn salvation, they always create rules to guard against sinning. They see that they can't obey the law, so they invent rules of their own to force themselves to obey. All this turns their minds away from God and to themselves. God's love fades from their hearts, and with it fades any love for others. The result is a system in which those who make the rules judge everyone who fails to live up to them. And this creates an atmosphere of selfish criticism that smothers kindness and generosity, turning people into selfish judges and spies.

This is exactly what the Pharisees had become. Their worship didn't leave them humble with a sense of their weaknesses, or grateful for the blessings God had given them. They were full of spiritual pride, thinking only of themselves, their

"Don't criticize and judge others, assuming that you understand their motives."

feelings, their knowledge, and their customs. They judged every-one else by their own lives, and with proud dignity, they criti-cized and condemned them.

The people followed the example of their spiritual leaders and judged one another on personal matters, on issues that should have been only between the individual and God. This is why Jesus said, "Don't judge other people, or you will be judged." He meant, "Don't set yourself up as the standard for others. Don't make your opinions, your sense of duty, your understanding of Scripture, as the rule for others and then condemn them if they don't live up to your standards. Don't criti-cize and judge others, assuming that you understand their motives."

"Do not judge before the right time; wait until the Lord comes. He will bring to light things that are now hidden in darkness, and will make known the secret purposes of people's hearts" (1 Corinthians 4:5). We can't read another person's heart. We can see only what's on the outside. Since we're flawed and defective ourselves, we're not qualified to judge others. The One who knows our motives, who can see into our hearts, and who loves us, is the One who is qualified to judge us.

"If you think you can judge others, you are wrong. When you judge them, you are really judging yourself guilty, because you do the same things they do" (Romans 2:1). When we criticize others, we're announcing that we are guilty of the same things. When we condemn others, we are passing sentence on ourselves,

> *When we criticize others, we're announcing that we are guilty of the same things.*

and God accepts our own verdict on ourselves.

JUDGING YOURSELF GUILTY

"Why do you notice the little piece of dust in your friend's eye?" (Matthew 7:3).

Even the sentence, "When you judge them, you are really judging yourself guilty," doesn't totally capture the seriousness of the sin of judging others. Jesus said, "Why do you notice the little piece of dust in your friend's eye, but you don't notice the big piece of wood in your own eye?" His words describe someone who is quick to see a flaw in someone else's life—and to point it out. But Jesus declares that this cruel character trait is "a big piece of wood" compared to the dust-sized flaw in the other person's life. It's a lack of self-control and love that leads a person to make a mountain out of a molehill. Those who haven't experienced a life-changing surrender to Christ don't show the gentle influence of His love. They misrepresent the gentle, caring spirit of the gospel, and damage the tender spirit of individuals for whom Jesus died. According to Jesus, a judgmental, critical person is guiltier than the person he judges because he not only commits the same sin, but is also guilty of being arrogant and critical.

A person who is guilty is the first to suspect guilt in others.

The character of Jesus is the only standard to be measured against, and anyone who measures people against himself is taking Jesus' place. And since the Father has "given the Son power to do all the judging" (John 5:22), whoever presumes to judge the motives of others is again trying to take Jesus' place. Those who want to be judges and critics are choosing to be enemies of God.

A cold, unforgiving religious experience, like that of the Pharisees, leads to real unhappiness. A life without Jesus is a life with no love and no joy. And no amount of hype and enthusiasm or busy "religious" activities or programs can make up for that. It may take real talent to quickly identify the defects in others' characters, but to those who do this, Jesus says, "You hypocrite! First, take the wood out of your own eye. Then you will see clearly to take the

We can't influence others to change until our own hearts have been refined and made soft and tender by the love of Jesus.

dust out of your friend's eye" (Matthew 7:5). A person who is guilty is the first to suspect guilt in others. By criticizing or condemning someone else, he is trying to cover up or excuse the evil in his own heart. Sin brought with it the knowledge of evil. As soon as Adam and Eve sinned, they began to accuse each other of causing it. This is human nature without the influence of Jesus' love.

Once a person starts down this path, he is never satisfied with simply pointing out the faults of others. If he can't shame or badger others into doing what he thinks they ought to do, he will resort to force. As far as he is able, he will force others to go along with what he insists is right. This is what the Jews did in Jesus' day and what the church has too often done since then when it loses sight of the love of Christ. Whenever the church finds itself without the power of love, it always reaches for the strong arm of government to enforce its teachings. This is the motive behind all religious laws that have ever been enacted and the reason for all religious persecution since the days of Cain and Abel.

Jesus doesn't drive people to Himself; He attracts them. The only force He uses is the power of love. When the church turns to secular powers for support, it is clearly without the power of Christ—the power of divine love.

No one has ever been rescued from a bad decision or lifestyle choice by scolding and criticizing, but many have been driven away by such an attitude and have closed their hearts forever.

But the cure to this problem lies with the individual members of the church. Jesus teaches that we must first "take the wood" out of our own eyes and give up on being judgmental before we can try to counsel others. Jesus said, "A good tree does not produce bad fruit, nor does a bad tree produce good fruit" (Luke 6:43). He meant that our critical spirit is bad fruit, and it shows that we are bad. We cannot make ourselves better or more righteous. What we need is a change of heart. And we must have a changed heart before we are prepared to speak to others about their faults, for "the mouth speaks the things that are in the heart" (Matthew 12:34).

When someone is in crisis and we attempt to counsel or advise them, our words will have no influence for good beyond the example of love we have shown. We must *be* good before we can *do* good. We can't influence others to change until our own hearts have been refined and made soft and tender by the love of Jesus.

When this change happens, it will be as natural for us to live to bless others as it is for a rose to share its fragrant buds or for a grapevine to show its purple clusters.

If Jesus is in us, we will have no interest in watching for weakness in others. Instead of looking for ways to criticize and condemn others, we will be ready to help, to bless, and to rescue them. When we deal with others who are fighting a weakness, we will remember how weak we ourselves are. We will remember how hard it is for us to find our way back to doing right each time we fall. We won't push another person further from God with our criticism. Instead, we will warn him of the danger and pain in his path.

If we think often of the Cross and remember that our sins put Jesus there, we will never try to compare our guilt with that of others. We won't take it upon ourselves to accuse or judge anyone. Walking in the shadow of the Cross eliminates the spirit of criticism and pride.

Not until we are willing to sacrifice our dignity—or even our life—to save someone, have we really removed the piece of wood from our own eye. Now we are ready to help someone with a problem. Now we can speak to him and touch his heart. No one has ever been rescued from a bad decision or lifestyle choice by scolding and criticizing, but many have been driven away by such an attitude and have closed their hearts forever. A gentle, friendly, sympathetic approach may touch their hearts and draw them back. If we let Jesus show through us each day, He will demonstrate the creative power of His Word. We will be a channel for His powerful yet gentle influence that can re-create those around us in the image of God.

PEARLS BEFORE PIGS

"Don't give holy things to dogs, and don't throw your pearls before pigs"
(Matthew 7:6).

Jesus is speaking here of those who have no interest in escaping the slavery of sin. They have indulged in so much that is depraved and addicting that their natures have become twisted, and now they are not willing to turn away from their habits or lifestyle. Christians don't need to spend time arguing with or being ridiculed by those who will not respond to the gospel.

A person hidden beneath hate and contempt, beneath crimes and addictions, may shine like a jewel when rescued by Christ.

Jesus never gives up on anyone who is willing to listen to the beautiful truths of the gospel no matter how deep that person is in sin. To tax collectors and prostitutes, His words were the beginning of a new life. He drove seven devils out of Mary Magdalene, and she was the last person at His tomb and the first one He spoke to on Resurrection morning. Saul of Tarsus, one of the most determined enemies of the first Christians, became Paul, the devoted minister and missionary. A person hidden beneath hate and contempt, beneath crimes and addictions, may shine like a jewel when rescued by Christ.

PROMISED THREE TIMES

"Ask, and God will give to you. Search, and you will find. Knock, and the door will open for you" (Matthew 7:7).

So that no one could dismiss or misinterpret His words, Jesus repeats this promise three times. He longs to have those who seek God believe in Him and believe that He can do anything. "Yes, everyone who asks will receive. Everyone who searches will find. And everyone who knocks will have the door opened" (Matthew 7:8).

Jesus gives no conditions for this promise except that we crave His mercy, desire His counsel, and long for His love. "Ask," He says. The asking makes it clear that we recognize

God is searching for you, and the desire you feel to find Him is the work of the Holy Spirit.

our need, and if we ask in faith, we will receive. God has given His word, and it cannot be broken. If we come to Him with true remorse, we won't need to feel as if we are presumptuous in asking for what He has promised. When we ask for the blessings we need in order to grow more like Jesus, God assures us that the promise will be kept. Knowing that we are sinners is all we need in order to ask for His mercy and kindness. We don't need to be holy to come to God, but we must want to become holy, to have Him wash away our sins and purify us. We may always ask, because our great need and helplessness make Him and His saving power a necessity.

"Search," He says. Don't search just for His blessing—search for Him. "Obey God and be at peace with him" (Job 22:21).

Search, and you will find. God is searching for you, and the desire you feel to find Him is the work of the Holy Spirit. Give in to it. Jesus is speaking for those who are tempted, those who have fallen into sin, and those who have given up their faith. He wants to bring them back to Him.

"Knock," He says. We come to God by special invitation, and He waits to welcome us. The first disciples who followed Jesus weren't satisfied with a quick conversation. They asked, " 'Rabbi, where are you staying?' . . . So the two men went with Jesus and saw where he was staying and stayed there with him that day" (John 1:38, 39). In the same way, we are invited to come close to Jesus and stay with Him. Anyone who longs for the blessings of God can knock at His door of mercy with confidence, saying, "God, You said that everyone who asks will receive. Everyone who searches will find. And everyone who knocks will have the door opened."

Jesus looked out at the people who had gathered to hear His words. More than anything, He wanted them to understand the mercy and loving-kindness of God. To illustrate their need and God's willingness to give, Jesus talked to them about hungry children asking their parents for food. He said, "If your children ask for bread, which of you would give them a stone?" He appealed to the deep, natural love parents have for their children. "Even though you are bad, you know how to give good gifts to your children. How much more your heavenly Father will give good things to those who ask him!" (Matthew 7:9–11). No parent with a heart could turn away a child who is hungry. What would they think of parents who would tease their children with a promise of food and then disappoint them? What parents would promise their children healthy food and then give them stones? So how can we dishonor God by imagining that He won't respond to the needs of His children?

"Even though you are bad, you know how to give good things to your children. How much more your heavenly Father will give the Holy Spirit to those who ask him!" (Luke 11:13). The Holy Spirit is the greatest of all gifts. The Creator Himself couldn't give us anything better. When we beg the Lord to have mercy on us in our time of need and to guide us by His Holy Spirit, He always answers. It may be possible for a parent to ignore a hungry child, but God can never ignore the cry of a needy heart. That is such a tender description of His love!

It may be possible for a parent to ignore a hungry child, but God can never ignore the cry of a needy heart.

This is the message from the Father's heart to those who feel that God has forgotten them in their darkest times: "Jerusalem said, 'The LORD has left me; the Lord has forgotten me.' The LORD answers, 'Can a woman forget the baby she nurses? Can she feel no kindness for the child to which she gave birth? Even if she could forget her children, I will not forget you. See, I have written your name on my hand' " (Isaiah 49:14–16).

Every promise in God's Word gives us a reason to pray, knowing that He has promised to answer. Whatever spiritual blessings we need, we can claim through Jesus. With the simple words and the faith of a child, we can tell the Lord exactly what we need. We can tell Him about our situation, asking for food and clothing, as well as for spiritual blessings and the assurance of salvation. Our heavenly Father knows that we need all these things, and He invites us to ask Him for them. God will honor every request for our necessities made through the name of Jesus.

When we come to God as a Father, we accept our relationship to Him as a child. We must not only trust Him, but surrender to His will, knowing that His love never changes. We give our lives to do His work. Jesus has told us to search first for the kingdom of God and His righteousness, and if we do this, He has promised, "Ask and you will receive" (John 16:24).

The gifts of the One who controls heaven and earth are available to His children. These are precious gifts that come to us through the Savior's sacrifice; gifts that will meet the deepest needs of the heart; gifts that will last forever; all given to be enjoyed by those who come to God as children. If we claim God's promises, asking Him in His own words, we will find great joy in His responses.

THE GOLDEN RULE

"Do to others what you want them to do to you. This is the meaning of the law of Moses and the teaching of the prophets" (Matthew 7:12).

After reassuring us of God's love, Jesus invites us to love one another, a principle that covers all human relationships. The Jews were worried about what they would get, about how to secure the benefits they expected to receive because of their proper behavior. But Jesus teaches us that we shouldn't worry over what we will receive but over what we can give. Whatever we would want others to do for us is the thing that we should do for them.

We should put ourselves in the place of other people and try to understand their feelings, their problems, their disappointments, their joys, and their sorrows. We can try to imagine being where they are, and then treat them the way we would want to be treated if we were in their shoes. This is the ultimate definition of honesty. It is another way of stating the law, "Love your neighbor as you love yourself" (Matthew 22:39). It is the essence of the teachings of the prophets and a principle of heaven that will be seen in everyone who goes there.

The "golden rule," as this teaching is known, is the real meaning of courtesy. And nowhere is it more clearly seen than in the life and character of Jesus. Gentleness, kindness, and beauty shone on His face and flowed out from Him to every person He met. And that same spirit will be seen in His followers. Those who follow Him will be bathed in the atmosphere of heaven. Their pure lives will be fragrant like the garden of God. Their faces will reflect the light from His face, brightening the way for those who stumble in darkness.

> *Whatever we would want others to do for us is the thing that we should do for them.*

If we truly understand the concept of a perfect character, we will show the same kindness and gentleness that Jesus showed. His grace in us will soften our hearts and strengthen and purify our attitudes, giving us a heavenly gracefulness and a sense of courtesy.

But the golden rule goes even deeper. Everyone who has been touched and changed by God's grace is expected to reach out to others in a way that he or she would want someone to share the gospel with him or her. The apostle Paul said, "I have a duty to all people—Greeks and those who are not Greeks, the wise and the foolish" (Romans 1:14). We know of God's love, and we have been given great gifts from God, so we are obligated to pass on these gifts to others, even the most corrupt and downtrodden people we meet.

The same is true for the blessings of this life. When we are blessed with money or material goods, we are obligated to help the sick and suffering, the widows and orphans, just as we would want to be helped if we were in their place.

> *If we truly understand the concept of a perfect character, we will show the same kindness and gentleness that Jesus showed.*

The golden rule implies the same truth Jesus had spoken earlier in His sermon—"the amount you give to others will be given to you" (Matthew 7:2). The way we treat others, whether good or evil, will return to us as a blessing or a curse. Whatever we give, we will receive back. The money or favors we give others are often more than repaid in our time of need. And besides this, all generous giving is repaid with a greater sense of God's love—the riches of heaven.

But it's also true that the evil we do to others returns to us as well. Everyone who feels free to condemn or mock others will eventually find the tables turned. They will feel the sting of ridicule or criticism because they had no sympathy or compassion for others.

Through His love, God leads us to detest our selfishness and open our hearts to Jesus. Out of evil comes good, and what appeared to be a curse becomes a blessing.

The golden rule is the true measure of Christianity. Anything else is a fraud. Any belief system that sees little value in human life—humans that Jesus loved enough to die for—and that would lead us to care nothing for human suffering or human rights, is a false religion. If we ignore the needs of those who are poor, suffering, or sinful, we are traitors to the love of Christ. The reason Christianity has so little power in the world and so many have even cursed God's name is because so many who call themselves Christians fail to act as Jesus did.

The reason Christianity has so little power in the world . . . is because so many who call themselves Christians fail to act as Jesus did.

In the early days of the church, when the memory of Jesus' glory was still strong, the believers shared everything, and no one was left in need. "No one in the group needed anything. From time to time those who owned fields or houses sold them, brought the money, and gave it to the apostles. Then the money was given to anyone who needed it" (Acts 4:34, 35). With true unity and love, they "ate together in their homes, happy to share their food with joyful hearts. They praised God and were liked by all the people" (Acts 2:46, 47).

Search heaven and earth and you will find no truth more powerful than acts of kindness to those in need. This is the truth as shown and taught by Jesus. When Christians actively live the principles of the golden rule, their preaching of the gospel will have the same power it did in the days of the apostles.

THE NARROW ROAD

"But the gate is small and the road is narrow that leads to true life"
(Matthew 7:14).

In Jesus' day, the people of Palestine lived in walled cities, most of which were on hills or mountains. The roads leading up to the city gates were narrow and rocky, and the gates were closed at sunset. A traveler rushing home at the end of the day had to hurry up the steep path in order to reach the gate before nightfall. Anyone who arrived late was left outside.

Search heaven and earth and you will find no truth more powerful than acts of kindness to those in need.

These steep, narrow roads leading to home and safety gave Jesus an impressive illustration of the Christian life. "Following the golden rule," Jesus was saying, "means that your path is narrow and the gate to enter heaven is small. There is a wide road, but it leads to destruction. If you want to grow spiritually, you must join the few on the upward path and avoid the crowds that will choose the downward path."

The whole world with its selfishness, pride, dishonesty, and lack of morals can take the wide road to death. There is room for each person's opinions and teachings, space for each to follow his own way of thinking, to do whatever his selfish heart wants. It isn't hard to find the path that leads to destruction; the gate to it is large, the way is wide, and our feet naturally turn in that direction.

But the road to life is narrow, and its entrance is small. If we hold on to any cherished sin, the entrance will be too narrow for us to enter. We must give up our own ways, our own will, and our evil habits if we want to keep on the path of the Lord. When we follow Jesus, we can't follow the world's opinions or meet the world's standards. The path to heaven is too narrow for the rich and powerful to travel while displaying all their possessions, too confining to the selfishly ambitious, too difficult for those who always take the easy route. It took hard work, poverty, patience, and self-sacrifice for Jesus to walk the path to our salvation, and it will take the same for us to follow Him to heaven.

The downward road may be decorated with flowers, but there are thorns in the path.

But we shouldn't necessarily conclude that the upward path is hard and the downward one easy. The road to death includes pain, sorrow, and disappointment as warnings not to proceed. God's love makes it hard for the reckless and stubborn to destroy themselves. Satan's path does appear attractive, but it's an illusion. It is a place of pain, regret, and disappointment. Selfish, ambitious plans may seem exciting, but that path will poison our happiness and destroy our hope. The downward road may be decorated with flowers, but there are thorns in the path. What begins as hope and excitement fades into gloomy depression, and the person who follows this path descends into a dark night that never ends.

With each step, we will be more able to feel His touch, and more of His glory will shine upon our path.

"The lives of those who are not trustworthy are hard" (Proverbs

13:15), but "wisdom will make your life pleasant and will bring you peace" (Proverbs 3:17). Every time we follow Jesus' example, every time we act selflessly for His sake, every trouble we endure, every temptation we resist, is a step on the upward path to heaven. If we choose Jesus to guide us, He will lead us safely. Not even the weakest person is in danger of failure when he or she follows Jesus. That path may be so narrow, so holy that sin cannot be allowed there, but everyone is welcome to follow it. Not even the most doubting, frightened sinner can ever say, "God does not care about me."

We cannot, by ourselves, overcome the evil impulses and habits that want to control our lives.

The road ahead may be rough and steep. There may be dangers on both sides. We may have to work hard even when we are exhausted. We may have to fight on even when we are weak, holding on to hope even when we are discouraged. But with Jesus as our Guide, we will not fail to reach our destination. Jesus Himself walked this rough way before us, and He has smoothed the path for our feet.

There will be reasons for joy all the way along the steep path leading to heaven. When we are guided by wisdom, we will find happiness even in the difficult times, because Jesus walks invisibly beside us. With each step, we will be more able to feel His touch, and more of His glory will shine upon our path. Our songs of praise will rise to join the songs of angels at God's throne. "The way of the good person is like the light of dawn, growing brighter and brighter until full daylight" (Proverbs 4:18).

OVERCOMING OUR SELFISH NATURE

"Try hard to enter through the narrow door" (Luke 13:24).

The traveler rushing home at the end of the day to reach the city gates before the sun went down didn't stop for anything. He was completely focused on getting inside the gate. "We must have the same kind of focus in the Christian life," Jesus is saying. "I have shown you the beauty of a developed character, the true glory of My kingdom. It doesn't offer you political power, but it is worthy of your best effort. It's not a fight for control over the earth, but don't think that it doesn't require a battle. My kingdom is worth all your best work, all your struggles."

The Christian life is an ongoing battle. But it's not a fight that can be won by human effort. The battleground for this war is the human heart and mind. And the battle we must fight—the greatest battle ever fought by humankind—is the surrender of our hearts to God's will. Our old human nature cannot inherit God's kingdom. We must give up our inherited tendency to selfishness and our old habits.

We can't hold on to self and selfishness and still enter God's kingdom.

When we are determined to enter God's spiritual kingdom, we will find that the power and passion of our sinful natures, backed by the forces of darkness, fight against us. Our natural selfishness and pride will fight against anything that would demonstrate their sinfulness. We cannot, by ourselves, overcome the evil impulses and habits that want to control our lives. We cannot escape the clutches of Satan. Only God can rescue us.

But He cannot work to change us without our consent and our cooperation. The Holy Spirit works through our senses and abilities, so we must work with God to change.

This is a battle we will not win without sincere prayer and humility. We must willingly submit ourselves to God because He will never force us to cooperate with Him. If it were possible to increase the intensity of the Holy Spirit's influence one hundred times, this still wouldn't make us good enough to live in heaven. We must choose to put our will on God's side. We are not able, by ourselves, to surrender our desires and ideals and our preferences to God. But if we are "willing to be made willing" to surrender, God will do the work for us, helping us to "capture every thought and make it give up and obey Christ" (2 Corinthians 10:5). The Bible says, "Keep on working to complete your salvation with fear and trembling, because God is working in you to help you want to do and be able to do what pleases him" (Philippians 2:12, 13).

We must be careful who we listen to. There will be people who try to lead us away from God and off the narrow path.

Many find the stories of Jesus and the wonders of heaven attractive, but they shy away from what they have to do to become true believers. They walk the wide downward path, but aren't really happy with their choice. They want to escape their slavery to sin, and through force of will, they try to overcome sinful habits. They look longingly at the narrow, upward way, but their selfishness, pride, and ambition stand between them and the Savior. They hesitate at the sacrifice it would take to give up their own will and the possessions and behaviors they love. "Many people will try to enter there, but they will not be able" (Luke 13:24). They want to do the right thing, they make an effort to do the right thing, but they don't really choose the right. They aren't willing to give up whatever it takes to enter God's kingdom.

Our only hope to overcome our own selfish nature is to unite our will with God's will and work together with Him every hour of every day. We can't hold on to self and selfishness and still enter God's kingdom. We can achieve holiness only by giving up self and accepting the mind of Christ. Pride and self-reliance must be crucified. Are we willing to pay that price? Are we willing to bring our will into perfect alignment with God's will? Until we are willing, God's love cannot change us.

The war we fight is the "good fight of faith." The apostle Paul says, "I work and struggle, using Christ's great strength that works so powerfully in me" (Colossians 1:29).

When Jacob faced the greatest crisis of his life, he stopped to pray. He wanted only one thing—to become a better person, to transform his character. But while he was praying, Someone—an enemy, he assumed—grabbed him, and he spent the rest of the night fighting for his life. But the threat to his life didn't alter his desire to be a changed person. When Jacob was exhausted, the Angel—Jesus—touched him with divine power and dislocated his hip. Helpless now, Jacob recognized his opponent and begged for a blessing. He refused to let go without one. Jesus blessed Jacob and gave him a new name: "Your name will now be Israel, because you have wrestled with God and with people, and you have won" (Genesis 32:28). In spite of his strength, Jacob could not win until he surrendered. "This is the victory that conquers the world—our faith" (1 John 5:4).

BE CAREFUL WHO YOU LISTEN TO

"Be careful of false prophets" (Matthew 7:15).

We must be careful who we listen to. There will be people who try to lead us away from God and off the narrow path. They may appear to be Christians, but inside they are destroyers. Jesus gives us a test to identify them: "You will know these people by what they do. Grapes don't come from thornbushes, and figs don't come from thorny weeds" (Matthew 7:16).

We can't judge a person by their words or the impression they make. We can judge them only by the Word of God. "You should follow the teachings and the agreement with the Lord. The mediums and fortune-tellers do not speak the word of the Lord, so their words are worth nothing" (Isaiah 8:20). The question to ask is, "Does this person's message and teaching lead me closer to God? Does he encourage me to show my love for God

Just claiming to be a believer means nothing.

by following His way?" When humans see no value in the moral law, when they pay no attention to God's commands, they turn their backs on heaven. They are doing the work of Satan.

Not all who claim to be Christians are true followers. "Not all those who say that I am their Lord will enter the kingdom of heaven. . . . On the last day many people will say to me, 'Lord, Lord, we spoke for you, and through you we forced out demons and did many miracles.' Then I will tell them clearly, 'Get away from me, you who do evil. I never knew you' " (Matthew 7:21–23).

There are people who believe they are right no matter how wrong they are. While they claim to be followers of Jesus and claim to do great things in His name, they are actually promoting evil. "With their mouths they tell me they love me, but their hearts desire their selfish profits. To your people you are nothing more than a singer who sings love songs and has a beautiful voice and plays a musical instrument well. They hear your words, but they will not obey them" (Ezekiel 33:31, 32).

Just claiming to be a believer means nothing. A saving faith in Jesus is not what many suggest it is. "Just believe," they say, "and you don't need to keep the law." But a belief system that does not lead to a changed, unselfish life is false. The apostle John says, "Anyone who says, 'I know God,' but does not obey God's commands is a liar, and the truth is not in that person" (1 John 2:4). Don't think that fortunate coincidences or miracles prove that a person's work or ideas are genuine. When someone gives his own thoughts and feelings as much authority as God's Word, we can be sure that he is not inspired by God.

Obedience marks the true disciple. We show whether or not we really believe what we say about loving and caring for others when we keep the commandments of love. We will recognize the truth of God in the teachings we accept when they eradicate sin from our hearts, protect us from immoral behavior, and make us more like Jesus. When generosity, kindness, gentleness, and sympathy show in our lives each day, when we find joy in doing the right thing, when we lift up Jesus instead of ourselves, then we can be sure that we have the right kind of faith. "We can be sure that we know God if we obey his commands" (1 John 2:3).

BUILDING A HOUSE ON ROCK

"But it did not fall, because it was built on rock" (Matthew 7:25).

As Jesus spoke to the people that day on the hillside, they were deeply moved. The simple beauty in the principles He taught appealed to them. His solemn warnings struck them as the voice of God who can read hearts. His words cut to the root of their long-held ideas and opinions. Following His words would demand a change in both their behavior and in their thinking. It would set up a head-on collision with their religious teachers, because it would completely overturn the authority of the rabbis and the power structure they had built over many generations. So while many were touched by Jesus' words, only a few were ready to act on them.

Jesus ended His speech that day with an illustration that vividly showed the importance of living the way He taught. Many in the crowd had lived their whole lives around the Sea of Galilee. As they sat on the grass listening to Jesus' words, they could see the valleys and ravines that funneled the mountain streams down to the lake. In the summer, these streams often dried up completely, leaving only a dusty riverbed. But when the winter storms came, the streams became raging rivers that sometimes filled the valleys and flooded the plains, carrying away everything in their paths. Often, when this happened, small houses and shacks built on the flat sandy plains were destroyed and swept away. But up in the hills, houses were built on rock. In many places, the houses themselves were built of rock, and many of these survived storms for hundreds of years. These houses were difficult to build, and they were not easy to get to. But no storm or flood could destroy them because they were built on solid rock.

"Those who accept and follow my words," Jesus says, "are like the rock-based house builders." Centuries earlier, the prophet Isaiah wrote, "The word of our God will live forever" (Isaiah 40:8). Years later, Peter would quote Isaiah and add, "This is the word that was preached to you" (1 Peter 1:25). God's Word is the only unchanging thing our world knows. Jesus said, "Earth and sky will be destroyed, but the words I have said will never be destroyed" (Matthew 24:35).

True religion lies in following the principles Jesus gave—not in order to buy God's goodwill, but as a response to His gift of love.

The great principles of God's law—the actual nature of God Himself—are on display in the words Jesus shared that day. When we accept these words, we accept Jesus. When we build our lives on them, we are building our lives on Jesus. "The foundation that has already been laid is Jesus Christ, and no one can lay down any other foundation" (1 Corinthians 3:11). Jesus—the Word and the Revelation of God, the demonstration of His character, His law, His love—is the only Foundation on which we can build a character that will last.

We build on Jesus by living up to the principles in His Word. It isn't enough simply to recognize the value of doing good; we must actually *do* good. Holiness is not a blissful, out-of-body experience. It comes from surrendering our will to God and doing His Holy will. When the Israelites were camped on the borders of the Promised Land, they needed more than just information or songs about Canaan. Those things wouldn't give them the vineyards and olive groves. The land would not be theirs until by exercising their faith, claiming God's promises, and obeying His instructions, they went out to occupy it.

True religion lies in following the principles Jesus gave—not in order to buy God's goodwill, but as a response to His gift of love. Jesus teaches that salvation comes with the kind of faith that shows itself in acts of love and mercy. The followers of Jesus do more than just talk about faith—they live it. "The true children of God are those who let God's Spirit lead them" (Romans 8:14). God's true children aren't those who are merely touched by the Spirit, or who follow the Spirit's urging now and then; His true children are those who let the Spirit lead them daily.

Do you want to follow Jesus but aren't sure where to begin? Do you find yourself in darkness, looking for light? Begin by following the light you do have—follow what you understand of Jesus' teachings in the Bible. His life-changing power is in His Word. Accept His words with faith, and they will give you the power to obey. If you live faithfully according to what you know, you will learn more.

Building all our hopes on our own selves is the same as building a house on sand.

You are building your character on God's Word, and as you do so, you will become more and more like Jesus.

Jesus, our Foundation, is like solid rock. His life goes out to all who build on Him. The Bible says, "You also are like living stones, so let yourselves be used to build a spiritual temple" (1 Peter 2:5). "That whole building is joined together in Christ. He makes it grow and become a holy temple in the Lord" (Ephesians 2:21). We, the living stones, become one with the Foundation—Jesus. And that is a building no storm can destroy.

But if we build on any other foundation, we will fall. If we build on a foundation of human ideas and opinions, of human rituals and ceremonies, or on anything we can do without the love of Jesus, then we have built on a foundation of sand. When the fierce storms of temptation come, we will be swept away. "This is what the Lord GOD says: . . . 'I will use justice as a measuring line and goodness as the standard. The lies you hide behind will be destroyed as if by hail. They will be washed away as if in a flood' " (Isaiah 28:16, 17).

Today God pleads with us: " 'As surely as I live, I do not want any who are wicked to die. I want them to stop doing evil and live. Stop! Stop your wicked ways! You don't want to die, do you?' " (Ezekiel 33:11). The same Voice we hear today spoke in anguish over the city of Jerusalem: "Jerusalem, Jerusalem! You kill the prophets and stone to death those who are sent to you. Many times I wanted to gather your people as a hen gathers her chicks under her wings, but you would not let me. Now your house is left completely empty" (Luke 13:34, 35).

Jesus saw Jerusalem as a symbol of the world that had rejected and hated His love. That day He was weeping for us! Even as Jesus' tears flowed, the people of Jerusalem could have repented and escaped destruction. For a short time, Jesus waited and hoped. He does the same for us today: "Here I am! I stand at the door and knock. If you hear my voice and open the door, I will come in and eat with you, and you will eat with me" (Revelation 3:20). "I tell you that the 'right time' is now, and the 'day of salvation' is now" (2 Corinthians 6:2).

Building all our hopes on our own selves is the same as building a house on sand. But it's not too late to escape the coming destruction. Before the storm begins, run to the real Foundation—Jesus.

"Because of these things, this is what the Lord GOD says: 'I will put a stone in the ground in Jerusalem, a tested stone. Everything will be built on this important and precious rock. Anyone who trusts in it will never be disappointed' " (Isaiah 28:16).

"All people everywhere, follow me and be saved. I am God. There is no other God" (Isaiah 45:22).

"So don't worry, because I am with you. Don't be afraid, because I am your God. I will make you strong and will help you; I will support you with my right hand that saves you" (Isaiah 41:10).